Welcome

52

109

63

Putting the yearbook together is always a pleasure – it's great flicking through everything we've done in the past year, reading all the feedback from you guys and picking out all the very best bits. We're covering all the usual bases, but have divided it seasonally this time – you've got gorgeous baking recipes, savoury snacks, party food and all the usual categories of wonderful food from all over the world. Some of the recipes are mine, but we've also got some recipes from our brilliant contributors, so big love to them. Enjoy these recipes, but also keep an eye out for more great things to come – we've got a cracking year planned. I'm excited.

Editor at Large

We've had another fantastic year of cooking and eating at *Jamie Magazine*. Choosing our favourite recipes for this yearbook is always fun – arguing about which is our favourite cake or pasta, and then deciding to put them both in anyway. Dividing the book up seasonally is something different for us. We've thought about when we would want to eat some things. Would we want all earthy, comforting flavours in winter, or should we spice things up with fiery South-East Asian dishes? Should we include some warming meals for the unpredictable British summer? After all, you can get many ingredients year-round in supermarkets. That being said, we've been very much guided by what's available, so look out for asparagus in spring, strawberries in summer and root veg in the cooler months. We're really happy with these recipes for all seasons and occasions, so you can cook up a storm for family and friends. Happy eating from us all at *Jamie Magazine*!

Editor

Thank you to our four sponsors

3

Jamie Magazine

Fully interactive version now available on iPad

Subscribe for just £29.99 a year
jamiemagazine.com/ipad

ALL RECIPES TESTED IN THE
JAMIE OLIVER KITCHENS

Contents

Love Fruit... Love Nature's Finest

SPRING
in association
with
Nature's Finest

SPRING
is the season to feast on lamb, tender asparagus, peas, new potatoes, zingy rhubarb and chocolate treats for Easter

LEEKS These layered greens perk up a winter harvest and last right into spring. Hailing from the same family as the onion, leeks are more mellow in flavour, giving a lovely depth of sweetness to dishes

MINESTRONE PRIMAVERA

MINESTRONE PRIMAVERA

This is a spring version of the classic Italian soup - the addition of pesto brings out the fresh, light flavours.

Serves 4

- 2 tbsp olive oil
- 1 onion, finely chopped
- 1 celery stalk, finely chopped
- 2 garlic cloves, finely chopped
- 1 leek, finely sliced
- 1 carrot, finely diced
- 1 courgette, finely chopped
- 1 litre chicken stock
- 120g stellette
- A handful of vegetables, such as baby spinach, green beans, frozen peas, frozen broad beans or a mixture
- A spoonful of pesto, to serve

1 Heat the olive oil in a large pan over a medium heat. Very gently sauté the onion, celery, garlic, leek and carrot for 10 minutes until softened and just beginning to colour. Add the courgette and chicken stock, then simmer gently for 5 minutes. Add the stellette, cook for a further 5 minutes, then add a handful of vegetables. Cook for a couple of minutes and season. Serve the soup topped with a spoonful of pesto.

SOPA AL CUARTO DE HORA

Fifteen-minute soup
Recipe by Elisabeth Luard
Serves 1

- 300ml ham or chicken stock
- 1 tbsp diced serrano ham, or parma ham or lean bacon
- 45g (2 nests) vermicelli or angel-hair pasta
- A few strands of saffron (optional)
- 1 hard-boiled egg, diced
- 1 chilli, deseeded and sliced (optional)
- 1 tsp finely chopped parsley
- 3-4 mint leaves, chopped

1 Bring the stock to the boil in a small pan, then add the ham, pasta and saffron, if using. Return to the boil, fork the pasta to separate it, then reduce the heat and simmer for 5-6 minutes, until the pasta is tender. You won't need salt.
2 Add the egg and chilli, if using, and simmer for another 2-3 minutes. Off the heat, stir in the parsley and mint.

SMOKED SALMON & RICOTTA PIZZA

Coating
- 60g flour, seasoned well
- 3 eggs, lightly beaten
- 100g panko breadcrumbs

Garlicky mayo
- 170g mayonnaise
- 1 tbsp finely grated garlic

1 First, clean all the mushrooms by brushing off any dirt, then trim them of any hard, woody stalks.
2 For the coating, tip the seasoned flour onto a plate, add the beaten eggs to a shallow bowl and pop the breadcrumbs onto another plate.
3 For the garlicky mayo, mix the mayonnaise and garlic in a small bowl till combined, then set aside.
4 It's easiest to cook the mushrooms in batches. Dredge each one in seasoned flour, the beaten egg, then breadcrumbs. Heat a few centimetres of oil in a large, deep frying pan. Once hot, very carefully fry the mushrooms in batches till golden and crisp. Carefully transfer to a kitchen towel to drain. Once the mushrooms are done, fry the parsley till crisp. Serve the mushrooms with the Tabasco for seasoning, and the garlicky mayo for dipping, and garnish with fried parsley

SMOKED SALMON & RICOTTA PIZZA

Spelt is great for pizza bases, giving a grainier texture and nutty taste.

Makes 1 pizza
- 150g ricotta
- 1 shallot, diced
- 60g smoked salmon
- 2 tsp capers
- 50g rocket
- 1 lemon wedge, for squeezing over

Spelt pizza base
- 200g wholegrain spelt flour, plus extra to dust
- 2 tsp baking powder
- ½ tsp salt
- ¼ tsp sugar
- 100ml buttermilk
- 1 tbsp sunflower oil
- 1 egg

1 Preheat the oven to 200C/gas 6. For the base, combine the spelt flour, baking powder, salt and sugar in a bowl.

2 In a separate bowl, beat together the buttermilk, oil, egg and 100ml water, and add to the dry ingredients, mixing everything thoroughly until you get a dough. Roll the dough into a ball.
3 On a lightly floured surface, roll out the dough until you get a round base 1cm thick. Transfer to a flour-dusted baking tray and bake for 15 minutes. Remove from the oven, and top with the ricotta, shallot, smoked salmon, capers and rocket, and squeeze over the lemon.

GARLIC MUSHROOMS

(not pictured)

Serves 8
- 200 Paris brown mushrooms
- 200g button mushrooms
- 125g flat mushrooms, sliced
- 40g oyster mushrooms, sliced
- Vegetable oil, for frying
- A small bunch of parsley
- Tabasco, to serve, if desired

SCOTCH QUAIL EGGS

Serves 12
- 12 quail eggs
- 2 thyme sprigs, leaves picked
- 3 thick sausages, meat removed
- 1 egg, beaten
- 100g breadcrumbs
- Vegetable oil, for frying

1 Preheat the oven to 180C/gas 4. Cook the eggs in boiling water for 2 minutes. Plunge into cold water and peel.
2 Mix the thyme and the sausage meat. Divide into 12 equal pieces and shape around the eggs. Roll in the beaten egg, then the breadcrumbs.
1 Heat 5cm of oil in a deep pan to about 180C and very carefully fry the scotch eggs in batches for 1–2 minutes, till golden. Using a slotted spoon, very carefully remove the eggs and drain on kitchen paper. Place the scotch eggs on a tray and bake in oven for 5 minutes, till the sausage meat is cooked through, then serve hot or cold.

HAVE
WITH A
BEER

GRIDDLED ASPARAGUS,
SPINACH & BACON SALAD

GRIDDLED ASPARAGUS, SPINACH & BACON SALAD
Serves 6

- 700g bundles of asparagus, woody ends removed
- 4 rashers of smoked streaky bacon
- 250g baby spinach
- A good splash of rapeseed oil
- A squeeze of lemon juice
- 30g Berkswell or Spenwood cheese (see note)

1 Put a large griddle pan over a high heat. When it's hot, turn the heat down a little and grill the asparagus for 10-12 minutes, turning often, till nicely marked on all sides and cooked al dente. Finely slice the stalks and put on a platter with the tips.
2 Fry the bacon in a frying pan for 5-6 minutes until crisp on both sides. Add the spinach to the platter, dress with the oil and lemon juice and season. Toss it all together, crumble over the bacon and peel shavings of cheese over the salad. Serve immediately.
Note Berkswell and Spenwood are British ewe's milk cheeses, similar to pecorino (which you could use instead). They're available from Neal's Yard Dairy and other good cheese shops.

POTATOES WITH SALSA VERDE

POTATOES WITH SALSA VERDE
Serves 6

- 750g new potatoes

Salsa verde
- 2 garlic cloves, chopped
- 2 tsp capers, roughly chopped
- 2 gherkins, chopped
- 4 anchovy fillets, chopped
- 1 tsp dijon mustard
- 1 tbsp red wine vinegar
- 3 tbsp extra-virgin olive oil
- A pinch of sugar
- 1 bunch of flat-leaf parsley
- ½ bunch of mint

1 Put the potatoes in a pan and cover with water. Add a pinch of salt. Bring to the boil and cook for 15-20 minutes.
2 Combine the salsa ingredients in a bowl, adding the herbs last.
3 Drain the potatoes and crush with the back of a fork. Stir through the salsa verde, season and serve

ONION, THYME & GRUYÈRE TART
(not pictured)
Serves 4

- 300g shortcrust pastry
- 1 tbsp olive oil
- 2 onions, sliced
- 2 eggs, beaten
- 200ml single cream
- 50g gruyère, grated
- 3 thyme sprigs, leaves picked

1 Preheat the oven to 190C/gas 5. Line an 18cm tart tin with the pastry, add baking paper and baking weights, and blind bake for 10 minutes. Remove the baking paper and weights, then cook for a further 5 minutes. Set aside.
2 Heat the oil in a pan and fry the onions over a very low heat for 40 minutes.
3 Preheat the oven to 170C/gas 3. Spread the onions over the pastry. Combine the eggs, cream, gruyère and thyme, and season. Pour over the onions. Bake for 20 minutes until set and golden.

GREEN BEANS WITH TARRAGON VINEGAR
(not pictured)

Herb vinegars are a great way to liven up simple veg sides. This is inspired by a favourite side at Fifteen London. It can also include lightly pickled shallot.
Serves 6 as a side

- 40g tarragon, chopped, plus extra
- 400ml vinegar
- 300g green beans
- 2 tbsp extra-virgin olive oil

1 For the tarragon vinegar, put the tarragon in a pan with the vinegar. Bring to the boil and simmer for about 5 minutes. Leave to infuse, off the heat, for half an hour. Strain, making sure you get all the vinegar from the herbs. Cook the beans in salted boiling water for 3 minutes, drain and toss with a dressing made of 1 tablespoon of tarragon vinegar, the oil and some pepper, plus a little extra chopped tarragon. Store any leftover vinegar in a sterilised bottle.

GREEN BEAN SALAD WITH CAPERS & PARMESAN

SPROUTING SUPER SALAD

GREEN BEANS, CAPERS & PARMESAN

Serves 4-6

- 300g green beans
- 1 shallot, finely chopped
- 2 tbsp extra-virgin olive oil
- 1 tbsp red wine vinegar
- 2 tbsp capers
- 10g shaved parmesan

1 Blanch the beans in salted boiling water for 3-4 minutes, drain, and refresh in a bowl of iced water. Tip into a serving dish and set aside.
2 Combine the shallot, oil, vinegar and a little black pepper, toss with the capers and use to dress the blanched green beans. Scatter over parmesan shavings.

SPROUTING SUPER SALAD

Recipe by Honeybuns,
honeybuns.co.uk

This is best served when the glazed carrots are still slightly warm.

Serves 2

- 70g whole hazelnuts, skins on
- 200g chantenay carrots
- 2 tbsp maple syrup or runny honey
- 1 tbsp avocado oil
- 200g sprouting seed mix, rinsed
- 2 tbsp finely chopped flat-leaf parsley, plus extra to serve

Orange & honey dressing
- Zest and juice of 1 small orange
- 1 tbsp avocado oil
- 2 tsp maple syrup or runny honey
- 2 tsp cracked black pepper

1 Preheat the oven to 180C/gas 4. Toast the nuts in a shallow tin in the oven for 4-5 minutes. You need them to go a little darker to bring out the toasty flavour. Let the nuts to cool, but leave the oven on.
2 Wash and top the carrots, leaving small ones whole and slicing bigger ones in half lengthways. Bring a pan of water to the boil, add the carrots and parboil for 4 minutes, then drain. Transfer the carrots to a roasting tin and drizzle with the maple syrup or honey, and avocado oil. Roast for 12-15 minutes. Shake the tin to coat the carrots with the juice, then leave to cool slightly.
3 Mix the sprouting seeds with the hazelnuts, slightly cooled carrots and parsley in a serving bowl.
4 For the dressing, combine most of the orange zest with the juice, avocado oil, maple syrup or honey and black pepper. Pour over the salad and toss to coat. Sprinkle over the leftover orange zest and extra parsley for extra prettiness.

BOMBAY POTATO SALAD

Serves 8

- 1.5 kg salad potatoes, skins on, larger ones cut in half
- Extra-virgin olive oil
- 1 tsp cumin seeds
- 1 tbsp of turmeric
- 1 red onion, finely sliced
- Juice of 1 lemon
- 2 tbsp mixed seeds, such as pumpkin and poppy
- A large handful of parsley, mint and coriander, finely chopped
- A large handful of fresh peas

1 Preheat the oven to 190C/gas 5. Bring a large pan of salted water to the boil. Parboil the potatoes for 8-10 minutes. Drain, steam dry, then transfer to a roasting tray. Crush slightly with a fork, drizzle with the oil, then sprinkle over the cumin seeds and turmeric. Season, toss to coat, and roast in the oven for 20-25 minutes until golden and crisp.
2 Meanwhile, put the onion into a shallow bowl, squeeze over the lemon juice and leave to soak.
3 Toast the seeds in a dry pan and set aside. When the potatoes are ready, leave to cool a little then add to a serving bowl with the onions, herbs, peas and a drizzle of olive oil. Toss to coat, then scatter over the toasted seeds.

SEEDS IN SALADS Mix things up, and experiment, by adding seeds to salads – from sunflower, sesame or toasted pumpkin to mixed sprouting seeds, you'll get a lovely texture and flavour in your salads, as well as a healthy dose of goodness

EASY
SUPPER

SPAGHETTI AGLIO,
OLIO & SPRING GREENS

GNOCCHI WITH ASPARAGUS SAUCE

PEA & GOAT CURD PASTA WITH MINT

SPAGHETTI AGLIO, OLIO & SPRING GREENS

Serves 4

- 400g spaghetti
- Extra-virgin olive oil
- 2 garlic cloves, chopped
- 1 red chilli, deseeded and finely chopped
- 1 head of spring greens, rinsed and finely sliced
- Zest and juice of 1 large lemon
- A good handful of finely grated parmesan

1 Cook the spaghetti in a saucepan of salted boiling water, according to packet instructions.
2 Meanwhile, heat a drizzle of olive oil in a frying pan. Add the garlic and chilli and fry for a minute or so, until the garlic is just starting to colour. Add the spring greens and cook, stirring occasionally, for 3-4 minutes, or until the greens have wilted a little. Grate over the lemon zest.
3 When the pasta is done, drain and stir in to the pan with a splash of the cooking water to loosen. Squeeze in the lemon juice and serve topped with a drizzle of olive oil and a handful of parmesan.

GNOCCHI WITH ASPARAGUS SAUCE

Serves 2-3

- 200ml chicken stock
- 350g bunch of asparagus, spears trimmed to 5cm, stalks finely chopped
- 50ml single cream
- 50g grated parmesan
- 500g gnocchi

1 In a pan, bring the stock to a simmer and cook the asparagus stalks for 5 minutes. Add the spears and cook for 5 minutes, until soft. The stock should be reduced by two-thirds. Take off the heat, add the cream and cheese and season to taste with black pepper.
2 Cook the gnocchi in salted boiling water for 3-4 minutes, until they rise to the surface. Drain, then stir into sauce.

PEA & GOAT'S CURD PASTA WITH MINT

Goat's curd is available from the deli counter in most large supermarkets. However, if you can't find it, substitute with very soft goat's cheese, or crème fraîche

Serves 2

- 200g spaghetti
- 100g peas (fresh or frozen)
- 2 tbsp goat's curd
- Leaves from 2 mint sprigs

1 Cook the pasta in a saucepan of salted boiling water, according to the packet instructions. Add the peas to the pan 3 minutes before the pasta is done. Drain, then stir through the goat's curd and the mint leaves. Season with black pepper and serve immediately.

ASPARAGUS Eagerly awaited each year, the British asparagus season lasts from April to mid-June. It's delicious in pasta and soup, or simply boiled or grilled till tender, then served with a sprinkle of salt, a drizzle of good olive oil and a squeeze of lemon

SQUID INK RISOTTO

SQUID INK RISOTTO

Recipe by Jamie's Italian

Squid ink adds a lovely earthy flavour to rice. You can buy sachets of the ink from most fishmongers.

Serves 6

- 300g white crabmeat
- 1½ red chillies, deseeded and finely chopped
- Grated zest of 1½ lemons, juice of 2½, plus wedges, to serve
- Olive oil
- 1 small onion, chopped
- 120g brown crabmeat, passed through a sieve until smooth
- 400g arborio rice
- 120ml white wine
- 20g squid ink
- 40g pangrattato
- ½ tbsp parsley, finely chopped, or microherbs, to serve

1 Combine the white crabmeat in a bowl with the chopped chilli, grated lemon zest and the juice of 1½ lemons. Season well and drizzle over a little olive oil.

2 Heat a little more olive oil in a large, heavy-based pan and gently sweat the chopped onion for about 3 minutes, until softened but not coloured. Stir in the brown crabmeat and simmer for another minute.

3 Add the arborio rice and stir for 1 minute. Pour in the wine and bring up to the boil, then simmer gently until all the wine has evaporated. Add half a cup of boiling water, and stir in to combine. Continue adding water and stirring until the rice is cooked al dente. Stir in the squid ink and the remaining lemon juice, and season carefully.

4 Divide the risotto onto plates and top with some white crabmeat mixture and pangrattato, garnish with parsley, and serve with lemon wedges.

CHICKEN NOODLE SALAD

This is a brilliant work lunch, and a great way to use up roast chicken leftovers (you could use leftover roast pork or beef, too). Make sure you've got good containers with secure lids to transport your salad safely.

Serves 2

- 100g cooked chicken, shredded
- 50g (1 nest) rice noodles, cooked and refreshed
- 1 tbsp olive oil
- 5 coriander leaves, chopped
- ¼ cucumber, finely chopped
- 1 carrot, shaved into ribbons with a speed peeler
- 1 baby gem lettuce, finely shredded
- A small handful of sugar snaps, finely chopped
- A good pinch of mixed seeds, toasted
- ½ small bunch of mint, leaves picked and roughly chopped

Sweet chilli & lime dressing
- 1 tbsp sweet chilli sauce
- Juice of 1 lime
- ½ tbsp reduced-salt soy sauce
- ½ tbsp runny honey

1 Combine the shredded chicken, cooked rice noodles, olive oil and chopped coriander leaves in a bowl. Add all the remaining salad ingredients, toss to combine, and then place in your lunchboxes and keep chilled.

2 Combine the dressing ingredients in small jam jars and take to work with your lunchbox.

3 When you are ready to eat your chicken noodle salad, shake the jam jar to mix the ingredients then dress your salad. Close your lunchbox again and give it a good shake to coat. If you fancy having a warm salad, remove the lid from the jam jar and briefly heat the dressing in the microwave before pouring it over your chicken salad.

CHICKEN NOODLE SALAD

MUSSELS IN BEER

SALMON WITH MOROCCAN QUINOA & QUAIL EGGS

"Aside from being an absolute joy to eat, salmon is full of omega-3 fatty acids, which are really good for you – we should all be trying to eat more," says Jamie. "I've paired it with harissa and some herby quinoa for the perfect Moroccan-flavoured feast."

Serves 4

- 300g quinoa or couscous
- 1 preserved lemon
- 1 tsp cumin seeds
- 2 tbsp pistachios
- 1 fennel bulb, finely sliced, fronds reserved
- A handful of black olives, stoned
- ½ bunch each of mint and flat-leaf parsley, leaves picked, finely chopped
- Juice of 1 lemon
- Extra-virgin olive oil
- 4 quail eggs
- 600g salmon fillet
- 2 tbsp rose harissa or regular harissa, plus extra to serve

1 Add the quinoa and preserved lemon to a pan of boiling salted water and cook according to packet instructions. (If using couscous, add the preserved lemon and cook according to packet instructions.)
2 Meanwhile, toast the cumin seeds and pistachios in a dry pan till golden then bash with 1 tablespoon of salt using a pestle and mortar, until you have a rough spiced salt. (You won't need all of it, but it keeps for ages.)
3 Drain the quinoa and transfer to a large bowl. Stir through the fennel, olives, and most of the mint and parsley. Dress with the lemon juice and a good drizzle of olive oil, then season to taste.
4 Cook the quail eggs in a small pan of boiling water for 2 minutes, then run under cold water and set aside.
5 Heat a large nonstick pan over a high heat. Meanwhile, rub the salmon all over with harissa, then place in the pan, skin-side down. You want to get the skin super crisp, almost cooked through. When perfectly crisp, turn and cook for a further few minutes, until just cooked through. The whole process should take 15–18 minutes.
6 Spread the dressed quinoa over a platter. Carefully break the salmon into large lobes and scatter over the salad. Cut the quail eggs in half then dot over the salad. Sprinkle with the cumin salt, remaining herbs and the fennel tops. Serve with little pots of extra harissa on the side, for those who like it hot.

MUSSELS IN BEER

Serves 6

- 2kg mussels
- A drizzle of olive oil
- A knob of butter
- 1 large onion, finely chopped
- 2 celery stalks and leaves, stalks finely sliced
- 700ml good-quality British beer, an ale would be best
- A small bunch of flat-leaf parsley, roughly chopped
- Rapeseed oil
- Sourdough bread, to serve

1 Rinse and debeard all the mussels (you can get your fishmonger to do this), discarding any that won't close.
2 Put a very wide, deep saucepan over a medium heat and add the olive oil, butter, onion and celery stalks. Cook, stirring, for around 10 minutes, until the vegetables are soft. Add the beer and bring to a simmer. Add the mussels, shake the pan, and cook for 4–5 minutes, or until the mussels open (discard any that don't). Transfer the mussels to a large platter or bowl. Leave the pan of liquid on the heat and simmer until you have a consistency you like.
3 Add the parsley to the pan and give it a shake. Check the seasoning then pour the sauce over the mussels. Scatter over the celery leaves, drizzle with rapeseed oil and eat with sourdough bread.

JAPANESE FISH WITH PICKLED SALAD

JAPANESE FISH WITH PICKLED SALAD

In Japan, tonkatsu pork and pickles is a popular cheap and cheerful lunch dish. This is our fish version – really a big fish finger sandwich, with quick pickled veg and micro greens to give a delicate Japanese aesthetic.

Serves 2

- 2 tbsp flour, seasoned
- 1 egg, beaten
- 4 tbsp panko or other medium-sized dried breadcrumbs
- 2 x 125g sustainable cod fillets, or other firm white fish
- 1 small purple and 1 small orange carrot, or 2 small orange carrots, cut into julienne
- ½ cucumber, cut into julienne
- 3 tbsp rice vinegar
- 1 tbsp soy sauce
- 1 tbsp togarashi chilli powder or sansho pepper
- Olive oil
- 2 large slices of good-quality bread
- Mayonnaise, to serve (optional)
- Micro herbs and shiso leaves, to serve (optional, see note)

1 Place the flour, beaten egg and breadcrumbs in 3 separate shallow and wide dishes. Dip the fish fillets in the flour, then the egg, and then the breadcrumbs to coat both sides. Refrigerate the fish for at least 1 hour to help the crumbs stick better when you come to cook it.
2 Meanwhile, combine the carrot, cucumber, vinegar, soy sauce and chilli powder in a bowl, toss, and leave to marinate while the fish is chilling.
3 Heat a splash of olive oil in a large frying pan over a medium heat and fry the fish for 3-4 minutes each side, until golden and cooked through.
4 Spread the bread with mayonnaise (if you like) and top with the cooked fish. Sprinkle with micro herbs and shiso leaves and serve with the pickled vegetables on the side.
Note Micro herbs are available from farmers' markets, major supermarkets and finefoodspecialist.co.uk. If unavailable, use your favourite herbs, finely chopped. Shiso leaves can be bought from Japanese grocers or at japancentre.com or atariya.co.uk.

SEAFOOD & EGG CURRY

SEAFOOD & EGG CURRY

This unusual dish uses two of the 'three spices of Ayurveda': coriander and fennel (the third is cumin), which are claimed to help balance body and mind. We claim that this is the perfect curry for uncertain spring weather: lighter in flavour than other curries, but still with a satisfying spice hum.

Serves 4-6

- Groundnut oil
- 2 onions, finely sliced
- 1 green chilli, finely sliced
- 1 tsp fennel seeds
- 1 tsp ground coriander
- A pinch of ground cinnamon
- 6-8 tomatoes, roughly chopped
- 4 tbsp fresh grated coconut (if unavailable, use frozen grated coconut)
- 4 eggs
- 12 king prawns, shelled, cleaned and deveined
- 2 squid, cleaned, cut into 1cm rings
- 12 scallops, cleaned
- Naan bread, to serve
- ½ bunch of coriander, chopped, to serve
- 2 limes, halved, to serve

1 Heat a good drizzle of oil in a large frying pan over a medium heat. Add the onion, chilli, fennel seeds, ground coriander and cinnamon and sauté for 10 minutes until softened but not coloured. Add the tomatoes and grated coconut, reduce the heat to low and let it all cook gently for 10 minutes.
2 Meanwhile, gently lower the eggs into a pan of boiling water and cook for 7-8 minutes. Remove and leave to cool in a bowl of cold water.
3 Once the spicy tomato sauce has slightly reduced, add the seafood and a splash of water if the sauce is very thick. Cover and cook for a further 8-10 minutes, stirring once, until the seafood is cooked through.
4 Meanwhile, peel the eggs and cut into quarters. Stir into the curry and serve on warmed naan bread, with chopped coriander and lime for squeezing.

ROAST LAMB WITH LEMON POTATOES

potatoes and roast in the oven for 30 minutes. Turn the heat down to 180C/gas 4, spoon some of the pan juices over the potatoes and continue to cook for 1–1½ hours, or until the lamb is tender and the potatoes are sticky and dark golden. Rest the lamb for 15 minutes, then serve on a platter with the potatoes and some pan juices.

PORK SHOULDER STROGANOFF

"Instead of stroganoff cuts like beef fillet or loin, I've used good old pork shoulder," says Jamie. "Cooking it really slowly lets it develop incredible flavours as it gets tender in the oven."

Serves 6

- 1 x 1.5kg pork shoulder, fat removed
- 300g button mushrooms, larger ones halved
- 2 red onions, quartered
- Olive oil
- 1–2 tsp cayenne pepper
- A few thyme sprigs
- 200ml single cream
- 1 garlic clove
- 2 gherkins
- 1 small bunch of flat-leaf parsley
- Grated zest and juice of 1 lemon
- Smoked paprika
- Plain yoghurt and rice, to serve

1 Preheat the oven to 180C/gas 4. Place the pork, mushrooms and onions in a snug-fitting casserole with a glug of olive oil, the cayenne, thyme, a big pinch of salt and pepper and 300ml water. Roast, uncovered, for 3½ hours, till the meat is falling apart. Remove from the oven then shred the meat with 2 forks. Remove and discard any fat.
2 Put the dish over a high heat and reduce the liquid by about a third, till the sauce has a nice consistency; lower the heat and stir in the cream.
3 Finely chop the garlic, gherkins and parsley on a board, then finely grate over the lemon zest and toss to combine. Add half to the stroganoff, then squeeze the lemon juice into the remaining gherkin mixture and mix well. Taste and correct the seasoning then scatter it over the stroganoff, along with a pinch of paprika. Serve the pork stroganoff with rice, and yoghurt on the side.

ROAST LAMB WITH LEMON POTATOES

Serves 12

- 150g drained (280g jar) sundried tomatoes, roughly chopped
- 150g black olives, pitted and chopped
- 100g capers, rinsed
- 1 tbsp finely chopped rosemary, plus 3–4 sprigs for roasting
- 2 tbsp red wine vinegar
- 1 x 2kg butterflied leg or saddle of lamb
- 2kg potatoes, quartered
- 8 garlic cloves, skins on
- 1 tbsp dried oregano
- Juice of 3 lemons
- 2 tbsp olive oil

Confit garlic

- 6 garlic cloves, peeled
- 3 thyme sprigs
- 2 bay leaves
- Olive oil

1 For the confit garlic, place the garlic, thyme sprigs and bay leaves in a small saucepan. Add enough olive oil to just cover, and cook over a low heat for 20–30 minutes, or until the garlic is tender. Take the pan off the heat and, using a slotted spoon, carefully remove the garlic and place in a bowl to cool. Reserve the olive oil and use another time for cooking.
2 Preheat the oven to 250C/gas 9. Using a food processor or a pestle and mortar, blend the sundried tomatoes, black olives, capers, rosemary, red wine vinegar and the confit garlic to a paste.
3 Lay the lamb out on a flat surface and season well with salt and black pepper. Spread the paste over the lamb then roll it up tightly and tie at intervals with kitchen string.
4 Place the rosemary sprigs in a large roasting tin and sit the lamb on top. Arrange the potatoes and garlic around the lamb, sprinkle over the oregano and season. Pour the lemon juice and 100ml water over the potatoes.
5 Drizzle the olive oil over the lamb and

LOVELY FOR **EASTER**

LAMB & CHEESE PIE

LAMB & CHEESE PIE

Serves 12

- 7g dried yeast
- 650g flour, plus extra to dust
- 1 tsp salt
- 2 tbsp olive oil, plus extra for greasing
- 2 eggs, beaten
- Mixed leaves, to serve

Lamb & cheese filling

- 2 tbsp olive oil
- 1 large onion, thinly sliced
- 2 garlic cloves, finely chopped
- 6 spring onions, chopped
- 1.4kg boneless lamb neck, cubed
- 1 tsp ground cinnamon
- 100ml white wine
- 2 eggs
- 75g hard goat's cheese, grated
- 180g pecorino, grated
- 800g spinach or swiss chard, cooked, drained and chopped

1 Dissolve the yeast in 225ml warm water and set aside for 5 minutes. In a bowl, combine the flour and salt and make a well in the centre. Add the yeast mix, olive oil and eggs and stir with a wooden spoon until a dough forms.
2 Knead the dough on a lightly floured surface for 10 minutes, adding extra flour if it's too sticky. Lightly grease the bowl with olive oil then return the dough to the bowl. Cover with a cloth and leave in a warm place for 1 hour, or until the dough has doubled in size.
3 Meanwhile, make the lamb and cheese filling. Heat the olive oil in a large pan, add the onion, garlic and spring onions and sauté for 5 minutes, or until softened. Remove from the pan. Season the lamb and brown in the pan over a medium heat, in batches if you need. Stir in the cinnamon, then return the onion mixture to the pan. Add the white wine and 100ml water and stir well to pick up the crispy bits on the base. Simmer for 30 minutes, keeping a lid on for the first 5 minutes.

CHIPOTLE PORK SANDWICH

4 Meanwhile, beat 1 egg and stir into the cheeses. Lightly grease a 23cm springform pan with a little olive oil.
5 Preheat the oven to 180C/gas 4. Divide the dough in half. Lightly flour a work surface and roll the first piece of dough into a circle about 35cm wide. Carefully place into the pan and lightly press into the base and sides, leaving about 3cm of pastry hanging over the rim of the pan.
6 Spread half the lamb mixture over the base, followed by half the cheese mixture, then half the cooked spinach. Repeat with remaining ingredients.
7 Roll out the second piece of dough and place over the filling. Trim the edges, but leave about 4cm of overhang. Roll up the overhanging dough and crimp the edges.
8 Make a hole in the centre of the pastry lid. Beat the remaining egg and brush over the pie then bake for 45-50 minutes, or till golden. Remove from the oven and let cool slightly. Serve with a mixed green salad. This pie gives delicious leftovers, too.

CHIPOTLE PORK SANDWICHES

This sandwich, packed with crispy, crunchy, spicy goodness, is so easy to make, and a great way to use up leftovers from a roast pork shoulder.

Serves 2

- ½ carrot
- ¼ cabbage
- 1 tsp mayonnaise
- 150g cooked pork, sliced
- 1-2 tsp chipotle sauce
- 2 gherkins, sliced
- 2 crusty rolls, halved

1 Finely shred the carrot and cabbage, and mix together in a bowl with the mayonnaise, to make a coleslaw. Season well and set aside.
2 In a pan, combine the pork with 1 teaspoon of chipotle sauce, and warm through over a low heat. Taste, and add more sauce if required.
3 Stuff the rolls with the pork, sliced gherkins and your coleslaw.

Get fruity

Essential to your health and wellbeing, fruit should play a big part in your daily diet. Nature's Finest tells us why and offers some delicious ideas for making sure we always get our five-a-day

MANDARINS

Mandarins are a great source of Vitamin C. Just one portion provides 80% of your RDA (Recommended Daily Allowance). Not to mention that eating Mandarins and other fruits has shown to promote heart health. So why not...

Serve mandarins with fish such as halibut, flounder, rockfish or even salmon? The sweetness of the mandarins brings out the flavours in the fish.

PAPAYA

Just a small papaya contains about 300% of the RDA of Vitamin C. So why not...

Create a quick, healthy and extremely tasty stir fry with papaya and peppers?

PINEAPPLE

Pineapple is fat-free so it's a great snack option if you're watching your weight So why not...

Blend pineapple with yoghurt and coconut for a taste of the tropics? If you're feeling naughty you could add a drop of rum, too.

PEACHES

Peaches are an alkaline-based fruit, so they are great to aid digestion. In China the peach tree is considered to be the tree of life.

So why not...

Liven up a bowl of granola and yoghurt with Nature's Finest Peaches in Juice for all year round sunshine in your breakfast?

PRUNES

Prunes are a good source of Vitamin A, which is really important for healthy skin and hair, as well as bone development.

So why not...

Add to your stuffing with a hearty Sunday Roast?

PEARS

A medium-sized pear packs 6g of fibre, which equals about 24% of your RDA of fibre.

So why not...

Try Nature's Finest Pears in a delicious chocolate crumble pudding?

To find out more about Nature's Finest visit us at **spcnaturesfinest.co.uk** or on Facebook and Twitter.

SPC EST. 1918
Nature's Finest®

STICKY PORK NOODLES

BROCCOLI Purple sprouting broccoli emerges in early spring and is quite different from its more common, green calabrese cousin, which lasts well into summer and early autumn. Both are tender and rich in vitamins and iron; delicious, too

STICKY PORK NOODLES

Serves 4

- 350g pork tenderloin, sliced into 4-5cm strips (you can substitute prawns or tofu, if you prefer)
- 300g broccoli, cut into florets
- 4 mushrooms, quartered
- 410g fresh egg noodles, or 240g dried noodles
- 1 tbsp groundnut oil
- 2 garlic cloves, finely sliced
- 3cm piece of ginger, sliced
- 200g beansprouts
- 1 red chilli, sliced, to serve (optional)

Marinade

- 4 tbsp soy sauce
- 1 tsp five-spice powder
- 1 tsp chilli powder
- 1½ tbsp honey
- 1 tbsp rice wine vinegar
- A dash of sesame oil

1 For the marinade, mix all the ingredients in a shallow dish. Add the pork to the dish and set aside.
2 Cook the broccoli in a pan of salted boiling water for 2 minutes. Add the noodles and cook according to packet instructions. Drain, reserving a little of the cooking water, and set aside.
3 Heat the groundnut oil in a large pan or wok over a high heat and fry the garlic and ginger for 2-3 minutes, until golden. Add the pork (reserving the marinade) and mushrooms and fry for 3-4 minutes, until browned. Stir in the marinade and reduce the heat a little. Toss the pork and mushrooms to coat and fry for a few minutes until sticky and cooked through. Add the noodles, broccoli and reserved cooking water and toss. Once it's lovely and sticky, stir in the beansprouts for the final 30 seconds or until heated through. Scatter with chilli and serve immediately.

LENTILS, SAUSAGES, ONIONS & BROCCOLI

Serves 4

- 250g puy lentils
- 5 thyme sprigs, leaves picked
- 2 garlic cloves
- Olive oil
- 1 red onion
- 6 sausages, chopped into pieces
- 1 head of broccoli, cut into small florets
- ½ bunch of oregano, chopped
- ½ bunch basil, chopped

1 Place the lentils, thyme and garlic in a saucepan, cover with water and simmer for 25-30 minutes, till the lentils are tender. Meanwhile, heat a drizzle of oil in a pan and cook the onion for 5 minutes, until softened. Add the sausages and cook for 15 minutes, until browned. If the onion catches, add a splash of water. Add the broccoli and continue cooking, stirring frequently, for a further 5 minutes. Season to taste, then stir through the herbs and the lentils, and serve.

JAFFA CAKES

JAFFA CAKES

Makes 24 biscuits

- 1 egg
- 50g white caster sugar
- 65g self-raising flour, sifted
- Butter, for greasing
- 250g marmalade
- 100g 70%-cocoa chocolate, chopped
- Finely grated zest of ½ orange
- 2 tsp vegetable oil (optional)
- 1 tbsp water

1 Preheat the oven to 200C/gas 6. Whisk the egg and sugar with electric beaters until thick and creamy, then stir in the flour.
2 Grease a 12-hole jam tart tin and put 1 tablespoon of mixture in each hole. Bake in the oven for about 10 minutes, until golden brown, then remove to a wire rack to cool.
3 Once cool, cut the cakes in half horizontally, so you have 2 thin cakes.
4 Gently heat the marmalade in a saucepan for a few minutes, until it has thickened but is still spreadable. Sift to remove any peel, if you want a smooth centre. Allow to cool, then spoon a dollop of the marmalade onto the centre of each cake.
5 Melt the chocolate with the orange zest, oil (if you like) and water in a heatproof bowl over a pan of boiling water, stirring well. Cool until the chocolate starts to thicken, and spoon over the marmalade. Leave to set.

EASTER BEETROOT & CHOCOLATE CAKE

Serves 12

- 250g 70%-cocoa chocolate
- 3 eggs
- 200g sugar
- 100ml sunflower oil
- 100g flour
- 50g ground almonds

EASTER BEETROOT & CHOCOLATE CAKE

- 1 tsp baking powder
- 250g beetroot, grated
- 2–3 drops of vanilla essence
- 2 tsp icing sugar
- 2 tbsp cocoa powder
- 250g Greek-style yoghurt
- Mini chocolate eggs, to decorate

1 Preheat the oven to 180C/gas 4. Grease and line a 20cm cake tin. Melt the chocolate in a bowl set over a pan of simmering water. Beat together the eggs and sugar until light and fluffy. Gradually beat in the oil, followed by the flour, almonds, baking powder, beetroot, vanilla essence and finally the melted chocolate. Pour into the tin and bake for 40–50 mins, until risen and a skewer inserted in the centre comes out clean (cover with foil if it's browning too much). Remove from the tin and let cool on a wire rack. Meanwhile, make the icing by beating the icing sugar and cocoa into the yoghurt. Once the cake is cool, ice and decorate with little Easter eggs.

OREGANO POLENTA BISCUITS

(not pictured)

Serves 20

- 350g flour
- 70g finely ground polenta
- 100g pecorino, finely grated
- 2 tbsp finely chopped oregano
- 150ml extra-virgin olive oil

1 Blitz the flour, polenta, half the pecorino, oregano and a pinch of salt and pepper in a food processor until combined. Add the oil in a steady stream, and pulse until a soft dough forms. Lay the dough on a piece of clingfilm, shape into a 2.5cm-wide log and roll up. Chill in the fridge for at least 1 hour.
2 Preheat the oven to 180C/gas 4. Line a baking tray with baking paper. Slice the dough into 1cm pieces and place on the tray. Sprinkle with the remaining cheese and bake for 12 minutes, till crisp round the edges. Cool the biscuits on a wire rack and serve with cheese and chutney.

RHUBARB A sure sign of spring's imminence and a reason to get excited is the arrival of this stalky vegetable that thinks it's a fruit. Rhubarb leaves are infamously toxic but the stalks are fine to eat raw – not that you'd want to, as it's incredibly tart. Stew, roast, or poach it with sugar to bring out its natural luscious flavour

RHUBARB & ELDERFLOWER ICE CREAM

RHUBARB & ELDERFLOWER ICE CREAM

Serves 4–6

- 500g rhubarb, cut into 1cm lengths
- 125g sugar
- 60ml elderflower cordial
- 375ml double cream

1 Put the rhubarb in a pan with the sugar and cook over a low heat, stirring till the sugar has dissolved. Leave to simmer till the rhubarb is very soft. Take off the heat and allow to cool, then stir in the cordial and cream. Pour the mixture into an ice-cream maker and churn according to manufacturer's instructions, or place in the freezer and stir every couple of hours until frozen.

LEMON POSSET & RHUBARB

Recipe by Jeremy Lee

"These delightful little pots of cream made light with lemon, and lots of it, have a finish that belies their simplicity and charm," says Jeremy Lee, of London restaurant Quo Vadis.

Makes 8 small pots or glasses

- 500ml double cream
- 250g sugar
- 100ml lemon juice

Stewed rhubarb

- 6 stalks of pink rhubarb (or 2–3 stalks of the larger reddish-green kind), trimmed
- 1 strip of orange zest
- 1 vanilla pod, split lengthways, seeds scraped
- 3–4 slices crystallised stem ginger
- 4 tbsp white caster sugar

1 For the rhubarb, preheat the oven to 180C/gas 4. Cut the rhubarb into very small pieces and scatter over a shallow baking sheet. Add the orange zest, vanilla pod, ginger and sugar. Shuffle everything together then cover with tin foil and bake in the oven for 25–30 minutes, until the rhubarb is tender but not too collapsed. Remove from the tray into a bowl and set aside to let cool.
2 Meanwhile, place the double cream and sugar in a heavy-based saucepan and bring to the boil over a modest heat. Once bubbling, reduce the heat and let the mixture simmer, stirring from time to time, for 2 minutes or so, until the sugar is dissolved completely. Remove from the heat and stir in the lemon juice. Pour through a fine sieve into a jug, then divide between clean, dry serving pots or pretty glasses. Let the mixture cool to room temperature then chill in the fridge for at least 2 hours, or overnight, to set. Just before serving, top each glass of lemon posset with a spoonful of the stewed rhubarb.

LEMON POSSET & RHUBARB

PAYASAM

PAYASAM

Convert the rice pudding haters. Payasam comes in many guises in Indian cuisine. This creamed version is similar to rice pudding, and cardamom gives it a subtle, exotic flavour.

Serves 4-6

- 100g basmati rice
- 75g unsweetened desiccated coconut
- 75ml reduced-fat coconut milk
- ½ tsp cardamom seeds, crushed to a powder
- 600-750ml milk
- 50g jaggery (see note) or brown sugar, plus extra to serve
- 2 tsp ghee
- 50g each of pistachios and cashew nuts
- 50g raisins
- A pinch of saffron and gold leaf flakes (optional, see note), to serve

1 Soak the rice in a bowl of just-boiled water for 30 minutes. Drain, then add the rice to a food processor with the coconut and coconut milk and blitz to a grainy paste. Transfer to a heavy-based saucepan with the cardamom and gently stir in 600ml milk. Slowly cook over a medium-low heat, stirring constantly. Add a little more milk if it looks too dry. After about 10 minutes stir in the jaggery or brown sugar and cook for a further 10-15 minutes, until thick and creamy. Add more milk if needed.

2 Melt the ghee in a small frying pan. Fry the nuts and raisins until golden then stir through the payasam. Serve sprinkled with extra jaggery or brown sugar, saffron and flakes of gold leaf, if you like.

Note Jaggery is a coarse, dark unrefined sugar. It is available in the UK from Asian grocers, major supermarkets with a good Asian section or online from spicesofindia.co.uk. Edible gold leaf flakes can be bought online from ediblegold.co.uk.

TSOUREKI

TSOUREKI

A traditional Greek Easter bread.

Serves 15-20

- 300ml milk
- 20g fresh yeast or 10g dried yeast
- 80g butter
- 625g flour
- 1 tsp salt
- Grated zest of 1 orange
- 110g sugar
- 3 tbsp orange juice
- 2 eggs, beaten
- 1 hard-boiled red-dyed egg

Orange glaze

- 3 tbsp orange juice
- 2 tbsp sugar

1 Gently heat the milk in a small pan until tepid. Spoon 2 tablespoons into a cup and stir in the yeast. Set aside. Add the butter to the rest of the milk, stirring it as it melts. Set aside and allow to cool.

2 Place 125g flour in a bowl with the salt, zest and 1 teaspoon of sugar. Stir in the yeast mix, followed by the milk mix and beat to make a batter. Cover and leave for 20 minutes, till the mixture is bubbly. Add the remaining flour, sugar, orange juice and eggs, and mix into a soft dough.

3 Stretch and slap the dough in the bowl for 5 minutes, then turn out onto a floured surface and knead for 3 minutes. Place in a clean bowl, cover and leave for 1-1½ hours, until doubled in size.

4 Knead again for 2-3 minutes, then divide the dough into 3 pieces. Shape each piece into 25cm-long ropes. Pinch them together at one end, then braid into a plaited loaf. Coil the plait to make a round loaf and sit the egg in the middle.

5 Preheat the oven to 180C/gas 4. Line a baking sheet with baking paper, sit the bread on it and leave out for 30 minutes or till doubled in size. Pop in the oven to bake for 20 minutes.

6 To make the glaze, heat the juice and sugar in a pan over a medium heat until the sugar has dissolved. Brush the bread with the glaze, then return to the oven for another 20 minutes or until golden.

BATH BUNS

completely enclosed. Reshape into balls.
5 Place sugar-side down on the tray and cover with a damp cloth. Leave in a warm place for 30 minutes, till doubled in size.
6 Brush the beaten egg over the buns then bake for 15–20 minutes, until they are golden and sound hollow when tapped underneath. Just before you take them out the oven, warm the milk and sugar for the glaze till the sugar dissolves.
7 Transfer the buns to a wire rack and brush generously with the milk glaze while they're still hot. Top with crushed sugar and caraway seeds, if desired. Eat while still warm. These buns will last for 3 days in an airtight container, but you may want to reheat them before eating.

LIGHTER TIRAMISU
We've swapped traditional mascarpone for ricotta and reduced-fat cream cheese, which makes this a bit lighter and gives a delicious, delicate tang.
Serves 6
- 3 shots of hot, fresh espresso
- 100g sugar, plus 2 tbsp extra
- 400g ricotta
- 100g reduced-fat cream cheese
- 2 large egg whites
- 12 (about 100g) sponge finger biscuits
- A few splashes of vin santo
- 40g 70%-cocoa chocolate
- Chocolate coffee beans (optional)

1 While the espresso is still hot, stir in the 2 tablespoons of sugar, then pour into a shallow bowl and set aside.
2 Beat the ricotta, cream cheese and remaining sugar together for 2–3 minutes until silky. Whisk the egg whites until they form soft peaks, then fold into the ricotta mixture.
3 Get 6 small glass dishes or 1 larger dish. Soak 6 of the biscuits in the coffee, then break in half and layer into the serving dishes. Sprinkle with a little vin santo, then top with a spoonful of ricotta mixture. Repeat with the remaining biscuits, more vin santo and the rest of the ricotta mix.
4 Use a knife to scrape the chocolate into long shavings, or simply coarsely grate it, then sprinkle over the tiramisù. Decorate with chocolate coffee beans, if you like, and chill for at least 30 minutes before serving.

BATH BUNS
Serves 12
- 14g fresh yeast or 7g dried yeast
- 250ml milk, tepid
- 450g strong white flour
- 30g sugar
- 1 tsp salt
- 225g butter, softened
- 1 tbsp caraway seeds (optional)
- 12 rough-cut white sugar cubes
- 1 egg, beaten
Milk glaze
- 1 tbsp milk
- 2 tbsp sugar
Sugar & caraway seed topping
- 4 rough-cut white sugar cubes, lightly crushed, for decorating
- 1 tbsp caraway seeds (optional)

1 Stir the yeast into the milk and set aside. Combine the flour, sugar and salt in an electric mixer or other large bowl. Using your hands or the mixer's dough hook on medium, work in the butter till the mix is like fine breadcrumbs. With a wooden spoon, stir in the caraway seeds and yeasty milk until well combined. It will appear a bit wet, but don't add any flour. Rest the dough for 10 minutes.
2 Skip this step if using an electric mixer: grab a handful of dough, stretch it out and slap it back into the bowl. Keep doing this for 5 minutes until it's more elastic and easier to handle.
3 Turn the dough out onto a floured work surface and, with floured hands, knead it for 8–10 minutes (or 6–8 minutes using the mixer's dough hook) until it is smooth and elastic. Place the dough in a large clean bowl, cover with a damp tea towel and leave in a warm place for 1½ hours, until doubled in size.
4 Preheat the oven to 190C/gas 5. Line a baking tray with baking paper (or use a nonstick baking tray). Knock back the dough and turn it out onto a work surface. Divide into 12 equal pieces and roll into balls. Place them seam-side up and push a sugar cube into the centres. Pull the dough around the cube so it is

LIGHTER
ITALIAN
CLASSIC

GLUTEN-FREE COTTAGE CHEESE MUFFINS

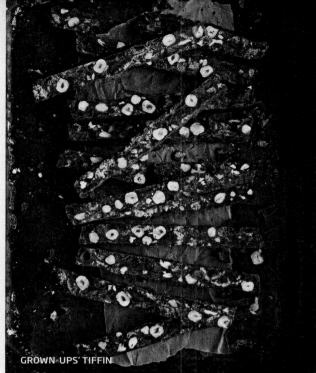

GROWN-UPS' TIFFIN

CHOCOLATE MOUSSE & FRUIT COMPOTE
Serves 8

- 150g 70%-cocoa chocolate, broken into small pieces
- 50g sugar
- 4 eggs, separated
- 150ml double cream
- 1 tbsp cocoa powder
- 9 tbsp apricot or cherry compote
- 4-5 tbsp brandy

1 Melt the chocolate with a tiny pinch of salt in a heatproof bowl set over a pan of simmering water (don't let it touch the bowl), stirring occasionally.
2 Meanwhile, beat the sugar and egg yolks until smooth. Whisk the whites with a tiny pinch of salt until soft peaks form. In a third bowl, beat the cream until it forms soft peaks.
3 Mix the cocoa into the egg yolks then fold in the whipped cream. Fold through the melted chocolate until everything is well combined. Tip in the egg whites and fold in until the mixture is smooth and evenly coloured. Spoon into a large serving bowl or divide between glasses. Cover with clingfilm and leave in the fridge for 1-2 hours to set.
4 Just before serving, gently warm the compote and brandy in a small pan, stirring well, then spoon over the mousse and serve.

GLUTEN-FREE COTTAGE CHEESE MUFFINS
Makes 12 muffins

- 225g plain cottage cheese
- 100g gluten-free flour
- 150g whole blanched almonds, very finely ground
- 100g drained sun- or semi-dried tomatoes
- 1 tsp gluten-free baking powder
- 75g parmesan, grated
- A few thyme sprigs, leaves picked
- 3 tbsp vegetable or other light oil
- 4 eggs, lightly beaten

1 Preheat the oven to 200C/gas 6. Line a 12-hole muffin pan with a double layer of paper cases. Put the cottage cheese in a bowl with the flour, ground almonds, tomatoes, baking powder, and most of the parmesan and thyme. Add the oil, eggs and 1 tablespoon of water. Season then lightly combine.
2 Spoon the batter into the cases and scatter with the remaining parmesan and thyme. Bake for 30-35 minutes, or until risen and golden brown. Serve while warm or at room temperature.

GROWN-UPS' TIFFIN
Makes 18 pieces

- 50g butter
- 200g 70%-cocoa chocolate, broken into pieces
- 1½ tbsp golden syrup
- 50ml whisky
- 90g amaretti biscuits
- 175g good-quality dried fruit, such as golden sultanas, sour cherries, cranberries and apricots
- 30g each of shelled pistachios and hazelnuts, chopped
- Cocoa powder, to dust

1 Line a 23cm x 16cm baking tin with baking paper. Melt the butter, chocolate and golden syrup in a bowl set over a pan of simmering water, stirring occasionally, until combined.
2 Take off the heat, stir through the whisky and crumble in the amaretti – not too finely. Mix in the fruit and nuts. Pour into the tin and spread to the edges. Pack it in well, and smooth the top down. Cover with clingfilm and pop in the fridge for 2 hours, or until set. Tip out, dust with cocoa and slice. The tiffin will keep for a few days in the fridge.

GIN & ROSEMARY FIZZ

AGUA FRESCA

GIN & ROSEMARY FIZZ

Serves 4-6

- 4 rosemary sprigs, rinsed, plus extra to garnish
- 20g caster sugar
- 80ml water
- 150ml gin
- Juice of 1 lemon
- 1 litre soda water

1 First make a rosemary syrup. Place the 4 rosemary sprigs in a small pan with the caster sugar and water. Bring to the boil over a medium heat then reduce the heat and let simmer for 5 minutes. Remove from the heat and allow to cool completely, then strain.
2 To make the cocktail, half-fill a cocktail shaker with ice. Add the gin, lemon juice and 3 tablespoons of rosemary syrup and shake well. Strain into glasses half-filled with ice, and top up with soda water. Garnish with rosemary sprigs and serve.

AGUA FRESCA

This is a version of one of South America's many 'fresh water' drinks.

Makes 1.5 litres

- 50g dried hibiscus flowers
- 100g sugar
- Thinly peeled zest of 1 lime (optional)
- Ice and lime wedges, to serve

1 Put the flowers, sugar and lime zest (if using) into a large jug or bowl, then pour over 1.5 litres freshly boiled water. Stir well to dissolve the sugar. Set aside to steep and let it cool to room temperature. Once cooled, transfer to the fridge for a couple of hours, preferably overnight.
2 When ready to serve, strain and serve over ice with some fresh lime wedges.

LEMON & GINGER CORDIAL

Makes 650ml

- 600ml lemon juice
- A large thumb-sized piece of ginger, grated
- 150g sugar
- 1 litre ginger beer
- 300ml rum (optional)
- A handful of raspberries

1 Pour the lemon juice into a medium pan. Add the ginger and sugar, then heat gently for 5-10 minutes, stirring until the sugar dissolves. Leave to cool, then strain into a jug. Add the ginger beer and the rum, if using, then pour into glasses filled with ice. Top with the raspberries and serve immediately.

Satisfy Your Taste For Discovery.

Come discover a pantry of inspiration surrounded by a feast for all your senses. We're less than a six hour flight from the UK.

Visit NovaScotia.com to plan your holiday today.

SUMMER
in association
with
Nova Scotia

NOVASCOTIA.COM
Freephone 00800 1565 0000

SUMMER

We love it! Abundant soft fruit, crisp salads, exotic vegetables... It's so easy to rustle up delicious dishes with a sunny twist

CHILLED AVOCADO SOUP & CORN CHIPS

CHILLED AVOCADO SOUP & CORN CHIPS

The summery flavours of this soup work beautifully with the spicy corn chips. Alter the amount of Tabasco, chilli and paprika to suit your taste, but remember the yoghurt will help keep things cool.

Serves 4-6

- 250ml vegetable stock, chilled
- 200ml plain yoghurt
- 1 large ripe avocado, flesh chopped
- 1 cucumber, peeled, deseeded, 3cm reserved, the rest chopped
- 4 spring onions, roughly chopped
- 3 tbsp roughly chopped coriander
- 1 mild green chilli
- Juice of 1 lime
- Tabasco sauce
- A handful of micro garlic chives (see note)
- 1 red chilli, finely sliced, to serve
- Avocado oil, to serve (optional)

Tortilla chips

- ½ tbsp olive oil
- ½ tsp hot smoked paprika
- 2 soft corn tortillas

1 Preheat the oven to 200C/gas 6. For the corn chips, combine the olive oil and paprika then brush over both sides of the tortillas. Bake on a baking sheet for 5 minutes, until golden and crisp. Season well and set aside to cool, then simply break into pieces.
2 For the soup, blitz the stock, yoghurt, avocado, cucumber, spring onions, coriander and green chilli in a blender until smooth. Season with lime juice, tabasco, salt and pepper, then cover with clingfilm and chill in the fridge.
3 Finely chop the reserved cucumber. Once the soup is chilled, serve in small bowls topped with the corn chips, chopped cucumber, garlic chives and sliced red chilli. Finish with a drizzle of avocado oil, if you like.

Note Micro garlic chives are available from larger supermarkets. If you can't find them, use chopped regular chives.

VEGETABLE BROTH & PEA DUMPLINGS

This recipe uses fresh green veg, cheeses and herbs to create a British twist to an Asian classic.

Serves 4

- 3 celery stalks, roughly chopped
- 2 carrots, roughly chopped
- 2 red onions, roughly chopped
- 1 fennel bulb, roughly chopped
- 3 bay leaves
- 10 whole black peppercorns
- A small bunch of parsley, chopped
- ½ small bunch of thyme, leaves picked and chopped
- Chives and pea shoots, to serve

Pea dumplings

- 150g fresh peas
- 50g ricotta
- 2 tbsp chopped mint
- 25g parmesan, grated
- Grated zest of ½ lemon
- 20 wonton wrappers
- 1 egg yolk, beaten

1 Make the broth by adding all the ingredients, except the chives and pea shoots, to a large pot with 2 litres of water. Simmer over a medium heat for 40 minutes, until the veg are soft.
2 Meanwhile, for the dumplings, cook the peas in a pan of boiling water for 2 minutes, drain, then refresh in cold water. Transfer to a food processor with the ricotta and mint and pulse until roughly chopped. Tip into a bowl, stir in the parmesan and zest, and season.
3 Lay out the wonton wrappers and put a teaspoon of filling in the centre of each. Brush the wrapper edges with the egg yolk, fold in half, press the edges to seal, then fold the two corners together.
4 Place a large bamboo steamer over a pan of simmering water, then, working in batches, place the dumplings on an oiled plate, pop it into the steamer and steam, covered, for 5 minutes, until the wrappers are translucent.
5 When the broth is cooked, remove from the heat, leave to cool slightly, then gently strain through a fine sieve into a clean pan. Avoid pressing the veg, to keep the stock clear. To serve, place 5 dumplings in each bowl, add the broth, and scatter with chives and pea shoots.

RUNNER BEAN & GOAT'S
CHEESE ON SOURDOUGH

RICOTTA & PINE NUT PANCAKES

BBQ AUBERGINE DIP

RUNNER BEAN & GOAT'S CHEESE ON SOURDOUGH

Serves 2 as a light lunch

- 1 tbsp olive oil
- 150g runner beans, finely sliced
- 2 spring onions, sliced
- 4 slices sourdough bread, toasted
- 50g goat's cheese
- 1 tbsp walnuts, lightly toasted and chopped
- Extra-virgin olive oil

1 Heat the oil in a frying pan. Add the runner beans and spring onions and fry for 4 minutes, until tender. Season, then pile onto the toasted sourdough. Tear up the goat's cheese and scatter over, along with the walnuts, and finish with a drizzle of extra-virgin olive oil.

RICOTTA & PINE NUT PANCAKES

These savoury pancakes make the perfect summer brunch.

Serves 4-6

- 250g large vine tomatoes, halved
- Olive oil
- 115g self-raising flour
- 240ml milk
- 1 egg
- A handful of pine nuts
- 125g ricotta
- A knob of butter
- 400g spinach, wilted
- A handful of rocket
- Grated parmesan, to serve
- 1 lemon, cut into wedges

1 Preheat oven to 130C/gas ½. Place the tomatoes cut-side up on a baking tray, sprinkle with oil, and roast for 3-4 hours, until dehydrated. Leave to cool.
2 In a bowl, whisk the flour, milk and egg with a pinch of salt until smooth, then stir in the pine nuts and ricotta.
3 Heat a little oil and butter in a frying pan over a medium heat. Ladle spoonfuls of batter into the pan and cook until golden on both sides, using all the batter.
4 Top the pancakes with the spinach, rocket, tomatoes, grated parmesan and serve with lemon wedges.

BBQ AUBERGINE DIP

Aubergines are a versatile summer favourite; serve this dip at your BBQ as an alternative to hummus.

Makes about 225g

- 1 aubergine
- 2 tbsp yoghurt
- 1½ tbsp tahini
- ½-1 garlic clove, crushed
- A squeeze of lemon juice
- ¼ tsp smoked paprika, plus extra to serve

1 On a hot barbecue or griddle, cook the aubergine for 15-20 minutes, turning, until charred and cooked through. When the aubergine is cool enough to handle, cut in half lengthways and scoop the soft flesh into a bowl. Stir through the remaining ingredients, taste to check the seasoning and serve, sprinkled with a little extra paprika.

CHEDDAR SCONES

TORTILLA CHIPS WITH GUACAMOLE & SALSA

CHEDDAR SCONES

Quick to make and easy to pack, scones are perfect picnic fare.

Makes 8

- 225g flour
- 1 tsp baking powder
- 55g butter, cubed, softened
- 50g mature cheddar, grated
- 200ml buttermilk
- Milk, for brushing

1 Preheat the oven to 220C/gas 7. Combine the flour, baking powder and a pinch of salt in a large bowl. Rub in the butter until the mixture resembles breadcrumbs. Stir through all but 1 tablespoon of the cheese. Pour in the buttermilk and combine. Knead briefly to form a smooth dough. Pat it out 1cm thick and cut into 6cm rounds. Brush with milk, and scatter over the remaining cheese. Place on a baking tray and cook for 12–15 minutes, until lightly golden. Serve with cheese and pickle.

TORTILLA CHIPS WITH GUACAMOLE & SALSA

Serves 8

- 1 tsp cayenne pepper
- 3 tsp cumin
- 3 tbsp rapeseed oil
- 8 flour tortillas, each cut into equal-sized wedges

Roasted tomato salsa

- 4 plum tomatoes, halved
- 1 garlic clove, chopped
- 2 oregano sprigs, leaves chopped

Zesty guacamole

- 2 ripe avocados, flesh chopped
- Grated zest and juice of 1 lime
- ½ red chilli, finely chopped
- 1 shallot, finely chopped
- A small handful of coriander, roughly chopped

1 Preheat the oven to 200C/gas 6 and line a large oven tray with baking paper. Combine the cayenne, cumin, rapeseed oil and a pinch of salt in a large bowl. Toss the tortilla wedges in the spice mix to coat evenly. Spread evenly over the tray then cook in the oven for 5–6 minutes until crisp and golden. Keep a close eye on them as they can quickly burn. Cool on a wire rack and leave the oven on.
2 Meanwhile, make the salsa. Roast the tomatoes and garlic in a small baking dish for 20 minutes. Remove 2 tomato halves from the mix, and blitz the rest, with the garlic, in a blender. Roughly chop the remaining halves and mix into the blitzed tomatoes, with the oregano.
3 For the guacamole, gently mash the avocado with a fork. Stir in the lime zest and squeeze over the juice. Stir in the chilli, shallot and coriander. Season and serve with the tortilla chips and salsa.

SUMMER ROLLS

Serves 12

- 50g rice noodles
- 100g or 6 large cooked prawns, cut in half lengthways
- 3 large basil sprigs, leaves picked
- 3 large mint sprigs, leaves picked
- ½ large carrot, sliced into thin sticks
- ½ cucumber, sliced into thin sticks
- 1 little gem lettuce, finely sliced
- 12 sheets rice paper

Dipping sauce

- 1 green chilli, finely sliced
- Juice of 2 limes
- 2 tbsp fish sauce
- 2 tsp sugar

1 For the dipping sauce, combine all the ingredients in a bowl and set aside for the flavours to develop.
2 Meanwhile, soak the rice noodles in a bowl of boiling water for about 15 minutes, or until soft. Drain and run under cold water until cool.
3 Fill a bowl with warm water and soak the rice paper sheets, one at a time, in it for 10–15 seconds until softened but not too soft or they will be difficult to roll. Place on a board and, starting with the herb leaves, arrange the ingredients down the centre of each, leaving space at the top and bottom. Fold the ends over then roll as tightly as you can. Cut in half and serve with the dipping sauce.

PACK
FOR A
PICNIC

SUMMER ROLLS

GREEN PANZANELLA

COURGETTE FRIES WITH TOMATO SALSA

GREEN PANZANELLA

Based on the classic Italian summer salad of tomatoes and bread, this recipe uses other summer vegetables for a fresh, seasonal twist.

Serves 2 as light lunch, 4 as a side

- 150g asparagus
- 200g broad beans, podded
- 100g mange tout
- 1 garlic clove, halved
- 1 tbsp red wine vinegar
- 3 tbsp extra-virgin olive oil
- 150g stale ciabatta, torn into chunks
- 1 fennel bulb, shaved, tops reserved

1 Blanch the asparagus, broad beans and mange tout in a pan of salted boiling water for 3 minutes. Drain (reserving a few tablespoons of the cooking water) and refresh in a bowl of iced water.
2 Roughly slice the asparagus. Rub the inside of your salad bowl with the cut side of the garlic. Add the vinegar, olive oil, seasoning and whisk well. Toss in all the other ingredients, sprinkle with the cooking water and add the fennel tops.

COURGETTE FRIES WITH TOMATO SALSA

Serves 4–6 as a snack

- 3 tbsp flour
- 1 tsp fennel seeds, crushed
- 2 eggs, beaten
- 250g breadcrumbs
- 1 courgette, thinly sliced lengthways

Tomato salsa

- 2 tomatoes, chopped
- 1 chilli, chopped
- Juice of 1 lime
- 10 basil leaves, shredded
- 1 shallot, diced

1 For the salsa, mix the tomato, chilli, lime juice, basil and shallot in a bowl, with a pinch of salt and pepper. Cover with clingfilm and leave in the fridge while you make your fries.
2 Heat a deep fryer to 180C. Combine the flour and fennel seeds in a bowl and season with salt and pepper. Place the beaten egg in a second bowl and the breadcrumbs in a third. Coat each piece of courgette in the flour, then the beaten egg, and then breadcrumbs.
3 In batches, fry courgette slices, drain on kitchen towel and keep warm while you do the rest. Sprinkle the hot fries with salt and serve with the salsa.

RATATOUILLE SALAD

Serves 4–5

- 2 romano peppers
- 1 aubergine, sliced into long strips
- 400g baby courgettes with flowers, sliced, flowers left whole
- Olive oil
- 90g tinned tomatoes
- 1 tbsp sherry vinegar
- 400g tomatoes, ideally a mixture of cherry and heritage, smaller ones halved, larger ones sliced
- 2 handfuls of mixed herbs, such as basil, chives or parsley, left whole, plus extra chives snipped into 2cm lengths
- A handful of mizuna leaves

1 In a searing hot griddle pan, grill the peppers on both sides until blackened, then transfer to a bowl and cover with clingfilm. Use the same pan to grill the aubergine, half the courgettes and their flowers until slightly charred. Transfer to a bowl, season, and drizzle with olive oil.
2 Carefully peel the seared peppers, tear into strips and mix with the aubergines and courgettes. Scrunch the tinned tomatoes in your hands and add to the bowl with the vinegar, and a splash of oil.
3 In another bowl, combine the remaining uncooked courgettes with the fresh tomatoes, herbs and mizuna, and season. Serve both salads together.

RATATOUILLE SALAD

Discover why top chefs make Nova Scotia their home.

Let's start with what's obvious to all who have visited us – Nova Scotia is beautiful. Chefs are artists, and like all true artists, they're not only inspired by their chosen medium – but by the places that surround them.

Perched on Canada's Atlantic Coast, Nova Scotia is renowned as a destination that stirs all the senses. From the Cabot Trail – named the most scenic drive in North America – to the endless white sandy coves, there is no end of treasure here. Our shoreline is peppered with vibrant villages and historical attractions. Majestic natural wonders like the world's highest tides in the Bay of Fundy, give way to gentler surf that sculpts our warm quiet beaches.

(Continued on right sidebar)

NOVA SCOTIA.COM

Freephone 00800 1565 0000

CRAB LINGUINE

RUM SCALLOPS WITH CHILLI & BLACK BEAN SALAD

CRAB LINGUINE
Serves 4

- Extra-virgin olive oil
- 1 garlic clove, finely sliced
- 1 tbsp fennel seeds, bashed
- 2 dried red chillies, crumbled
- 400g picked crabmeat
- Zest and juice of 2 unwaxed lemons
- 400g linguine
- 1 fennel bulb, finely sliced, fronds reserved

1 Heat a good drizzle of oil in a heavy-based pan. Add the garlic, fennel seeds and chillies; fry for 1-2 minutes. Add the crab to the pan with most of the lemon zest and all the juice. Season, and stir just enough to heat the crab. Set aside.
2 Meanwhile, cook the linguine in a pan of salted boiling water for 5 minutes. Add the fennel and continue cooking until the pasta is al dente. Drain, keeping a little of the cooking water, and tip the pasta and fennel into the crab mixture. Lightly stir, adding some cooking water to loosen, if needed. Serve with a drizzle of olive oil, and scatter over the rest of the lemon zest and the fennel fronds.

RUM SCALLOPS WITH CHILLI & BLACK BEAN SALAD

This sounds like an odd combination but the scallops and beans contrast nicely with the sweetness of the rum.
Serves 4 as a starter

- 2 tbsp butter
- 1 small red chilli, deseeded and finely chopped
- 8 scallops
- 50ml golden rum

Black bean salad

- 1 x 400g tin black beans, drained
- A small handful of rocket, lamb's lettuce, dandelion or chicory leaves
- 1 tbsp olive oil
- Juice of 1 lime, plus wedges to serve

1 To make the salad, mix the black beans, salad leaves, olive oil and lime juice in a bowl and season with salt and pepper.
2 Heat the butter in a frying pan until foaming. Add the chilli and cook over a medium heat for 30 seconds. Season the scallops, add to the pan and cook on each side for 3 minutes, or until nicely seared. Add the rum carefully and let it caramelise until it has almost blackened around the scallops. Serve immediately with the lime wedges and salad.

INDIAN CHOPPED SALAD

INDIAN CHOPPED SALAD

"I love the way Indian food brings out the wonderful perfumes and aromas in the spices," says Jamie. "I've embraced that, bringing a different texture and flavour to a chopped salad. Great to eat, and fun to make!"

Serves 6-8 as a side
- 1 tsp fenugreek seeds
- 1 tsp mustard seeds
- A small handful of fresh or dry curry leaves, crumbled
- Rapeseed oil
- 1 heaped tsp mango chutney
- 4 uncooked poppadoms (optional)
- 2 carrots, peeled
- ½ cucumber
- 4 spring onions, trimmed
- 1 bunch of radishes
- 2 little gem lettuce
- 2 big handfuls of ripe cherry tomatoes
- 1 red chilli, deseeded
- 1 bunch of coriander, leaves picked
- 1 bunch of mint, leaves picked
- 1 lime, for squeezing over

1 In a small frying pan on a medium heat, fry the fenugreek and mustard seeds and curry leaves in a big glug of rapeseed oil. Once the mustard seeds start to pop, stir in the mango chutney then remove from the heat and leave to cool.
2 Microwave the poppadoms for a minute or two to puff them up. Grate the carrots on a large board, then chop and add the cucumber, spring onions, radishes, lettuce, tomatoes, chilli and herbs, mixing and chopping as you go. Pour over the toasted spices, add a squeeze of lime, a pinch of salt and mix and chop it all up with your knife. If it's too dry, add extra oil and lime juice.
3 Serve sprinkled with crunched-up poppadoms, and extra dollops of mango chutney, if you fancy.

MEXICAN SALAD

BREAD, WATERMELON & HALLOUMI SALAD

MEXICAN SALAD

This is so easy to throw together, yet it packs a bright, zesty flavour punch.
Serves 4-6

- 2 corn cobs or 300g frozen sweetcorn
- 1 tbsp olive oil
- 400g tinned black beans, drained and rinsed
- Zest of 1 lime, juice of 2
- 1 pomelo or 2 grapefruits, peeled and cut into segments
- 1 romaine lettuce, chopped
- A bunch of coriander, leaves picked and roughly chopped
- 1 red pepper, deseeded and chopped
- 1 red chilli, deseeded and finely chopped

1 If using fresh corn, boil for 5 minutes, then shuck the kernels. If frozen, cook according to the packet. Heat the oil in a frying pan over a medium heat, add the corn and fry for 3-5 minutes, tossing occasionally until beginning to pop and blacken in spots. Set aside to cool.
2 Once cool, combine the corn with the rest of the ingredients in a large salad bowl, season to taste and serve.

BREAD, WATERMELON & HALLOUMI SALAD

This Greek-style bread salad combines sweet fruit with salty grilled halloumi.

Serves 6

- 2 heads of baby gem lettuce, leaves separated
- 2 handfuls of frisée lettuce
- 6 slices ciabatta, toasted or grilled and torn into chunks
- 400g watermelon flesh, cut into chunks
- 50g green or black olives
- 200g halloumi, sliced

Pomegranate dressing

- Seeds of ½ pomegranate
- 1 tsp pomegranate molasses
- 2 tbsp pomegranate juice
- 30g walnuts, roughly chopped
- 3 tbsp olive oil

1 Combine all the dressing ingredients in a bowl and set aside. Toss the lettuce, ciabatta and watermelon chunks with the olives in a bowl.
2 Heat a griddle or pan and cook the halloumi on both sides until golden. Add to the salad while still warm, drizzle over the dressing, toss to combine, and serve.

AUBERGINE & HUMMUS BURGER

This vegetarian burger might just upstage the beef at your barbecue.
Serves 2

- 4 x 1.5cm slices from the fat end of a large aubergine
- Olive oil
- 1-2 tsp dried oregano
- A tiny pinch of smoked paprika
- A squeeze of lemon juice
- 2 burger buns or wholemeal baps, halved
- 2 lettuce leaves
- 2 red onion slices
- 2 tbsp hummus
- 2 tomato slices

1 Toss the aubergine slices with a pinch of salt and leave in a colander for 30 minutes. Pat dry with kitchen towel.
2 Preheat a griddle pan. In a small bowl, mix 2 tablespoons of olive oil with the oregano and paprika, and season with a pinch of salt and pepper. Brush one side of each aubergine slice with some oil mixture and griddle them, oiled-side down, on a medium-high heat for about 3 minutes. Repeat for the other side. Keep oiling and turning every few minutes until cooked through and starting to char. Drizzle with a little lemon juice. Keep the aubergine warm as you griddle the buns, cut-side down, for a couple of minutes, until just warm.
3 To serve, lay a piece of lettuce and a slice of onion on each bun base. Top with an aubergine slice, followed by a dollop of hummus, then another aubergine slice. Finish with a slice of tomato, and finally add the bun top.

AUBERGINE When initially cultivated in Britain, the aubergine was a decorative, white, egg-shaped fruit and thus earned the name egg plant. These days it's more commonly seen in its deep purple form, and although it needs to be cooked, it's a versatile summer ingredient. Use cooked aubergine flesh to make dips, roast with tomatoes and garlic, or simply grill on the barbecue for a melt-in-the-mouth vegetarian option

AUBERGINE & HUMMUS BURGER

FENNEL Inherited from our Italian cousins, this sturdy bulb packs an aniseed punch. Its unusual flavour works particularly well with lemon, or fish. Beautiful in salads, baked with potatoes, or simply grilled on the barbecue

TALEGGIO, POTATO & FENNEL BAKE

TALEGGIO, POTATO & FENNEL BAKE

With our unpredictable British summers, a tasty bake with fennel is sometimes just what you want.
Serves 8

- 750g potatoes, thinly sliced
- 4 baby fennel, finely sliced
- 70g butter
- Olive oil
- 4 garlic cloves, finely sliced
- 2 onions, finely sliced
- A few thyme sprigs, leaves picked
- 250g taleggio, ⅓ sliced very thinly, the rest torn into rough chunks

1 Preheat the oven to 180C/gas 4. Cook the potato slices in a large pan of salted boiling water for 3 minutes. Drain and leave them to dry on kitchen paper.
2 Refill the saucepan with water, add a pinch of salt and bring to a boil over a medium heat. Once boiling, add the fennel and cook for 2 minutes. Drain and transfer to kitchen paper to dry.
3 Melt the butter in a frying pan with a glug of oil and fry the garlic till golden. Remove the pan from the heat.
4 In a deep baking dish about 30cm x 18cm, spread half the potato slices, overlapping. Season, then layer over half the fennel and half the onion. Sprinkle with thyme; add a layer of torn taleggio. Repeat with the rest of the ingredients, finishing with sliced taleggio.
5 Scatter over the remaining thyme leaves and cover the dish with tinfoil. Bake in the oven for 45 minutes, or until the potato and fennel are softened and cooked through. Remove the foil and bake for a further 15 minutes, or until golden and bubbling on top.

SPICY COLESLAW

This super-simple classic barbecue side gets a spicy West Indian spin with the addition of cayenne pepper and scotch bonnet chilli. Adjust the heat to suit your taste!
Serves 8

- 1 large cabbage, finely sliced
- 2 spring onions, finely sliced
- 4 large carrots, grated
- 5 tbsp mayonnaise
- ½ tsp ground cayenne pepper
- A handful of finely chopped parsley
- A bunch of chives, finely sliced
- ½ scotch bonnet chilli, deseeded and very finely chopped
- Grated zest and juice of 1 lime

1 Put all the coleslaw ingredients in a large serving bowl, toss to combine, and serve. Done!

SPICY COLESLAW

TROFIE WITH RICOTTA & HERBS

PASTA WITH RUNNER BEANS & PANCETTA

TROFIE WITH RICOTTA & HERBS

Serves 4

- 500g trofie pasta
- 2 handfuls of mixed herbs (basil, oregano, parsley, thyme, mint), leaves picked and roughly chopped
- Zest and juice of 1 lemon
- Olive oil
- 80g ricotta

1 Cook the pasta according to the packet instructions and then drain, keeping a cup of the cooking water aside. Stir through most of the herbs, the lemon zest and seasoning. Squeeze over the lemon juice, add a drizzle of olive oil, and toss again. Add a slosh of the cooking water if it's too dry. Crumble over the ricotta, toss together gently, divide between the plates and sprinkle each serving with the remaining herbs.

PASTA WITH RUNNER BEANS & PANCETTA

Paccheri rigati pasta is often served with chunky sauces, but works well in this summery bowl. You could use penne or rigatoni instead.

Serves 4

- 400g paccheri rigati, or other pasta
- 1 tsp olive oil
- 6 slices pancetta, chopped
- 250g runner beans, cut into matchsticks
- 2 garlic cloves, sliced
- A pinch of chilli flakes
- Juice of ½ lemon
- 2 tbsp grated parmesan

1 Cook the pasta in a pan of salted boiling water until al dente. Heat the oil in a pan and fry the pancetta and beans until the pancetta's crisp. Add the garlic and chilli, and cook for 2 minutes. Drain the pasta and stir through the bean mix, lemon juice and parmesan. Top with cracked black pepper, and serve immediately.

BUCATINI WITH ANCHOVIES & PANGRATTATO

This easy pasta dish can be thrown together using basic store cupboard ingredients, plus handfuls of chopped parsley, or basil, from the garden.

Serves 4

- Olive oil
- 3 garlic cloves, thinly sliced
- 2 dried red chillies
- 18 anchovy fillets, roughly chopped
- Grated zest and juice of 2 lemons
- 400g bucatini pasta
- ½ bunch flat-leaf parsley, finely chopped

Pangrattato

- 125ml olive oil
- 6 garlic cloves
- ½ ciabatta loaf, bottom crust removed, blitzed into coarse crumbs
- ½ dried red chilli

1 For the pangrattato, heat the oil in a small saucepan and add the garlic cloves. Cook over a medium heat until golden, then throw the garlic away – it's done its work. Add the breadcrumbs to the garlicky oil in the pan and cook for a few minutes until crisp and golden. Drain on kitchen paper, then season to taste and crumble over the dried chilli. Set aside.
2 In another pan, heat a little olive oil and gently fry the sliced garlic over a medium heat until it begins to colour. Crumble in 1 chilli, add the anchovies and stir to make a silky sauce. Remove the pan from the heat. Squeeze the lemon juice into the sauce and grind over some pepper.
3 Bring a pan of salted water to the boil and cook the bucatini according to the packet instructions. Drain and add to the anchovy sauce. Serve sprinkled with the lemon zest, the crumbled remaining chilli, the pangrattato, and the parsley.

BUCATINI WITH ANCHOVIES
& PANGRATTATO

COCKLE LINGUINE

JAMIE'S ITALIAN RECIPE

POLLOCK WITH RUM, COCONUT & CHILLI

SQUID, CHILLI & LEMON SALAD

COCKLE LINGUINE

Recipe by Jamie's Italian

A simple, summery seafood pasta – to be enjoyed with a glass of white wine.

Serves 4

- 1kg cockles
- 400g linguine
- Olive oil
- 2 garlic cloves, finely chopped
- 1 red chilli, deseeded and finely sliced
- 2 anchovy fillets
- ½ bunch of parsley, stalks finely chopped, leaves roughly chopped
- 1-2 tsp chilli paste
- 100ml white wine
- 40g butter
- Juice of ½ lemon

1 Rinse the cockles and test they're alive by sliding a small knife between the shells. If the cockle doesn't clamp down on the knife, discard it.
2 Cook the linguine according to packet instructions. Meanwhile, heat a glug of oil in a pan and gently fry the garlic with the red chilli, anchovies, parsley stalks and paste until soft. Stir in the cockles. Add the wine and cook, covered, for 2-3 minutes. If the cockles are not all open, cook for a further 1-2 minutes. Add the butter and parsley leaves, swirling the pan to melt the butter. Discard any unopened cockles. Add the drained pasta and lemon juice, stir well and serve.

POLLOCK WITH RUM, COCONUT & CHILLI

Serves 6

- 6 x 120g pollock fillets
- 250ml dark rum
- 125ml coconut milk
- ½ scotch bonnet chilli, deseeded and chopped
- Grated zest of 2 lemons
- A handful of chopped coriander
- 1½ tbsp ground allspice
- Olive oil, to serve (optional)

1 Rinse the fish in cold running water and ensure it's free of bones. Place in a wide, shallow bowl.
2 Combine all remaining ingredients in a bowl, pour over the fish, cover with clingfilm and refrigerate for 1 hour.
3 Heat the barbecue or griddle pan to a medium heat. Cook the fish for about 6 minutes each side, or until it flakes. Or, wrap the fillets in a double layer of foil with some of the marinade and cook on the barbecue for 12 minutes. Test with a skewer – it's done if the skewer is warm when you touch it to your lip. To cook in the oven, place fish in a roasting dish with some marinade, and cook at 190C/gas 5 for 12 minutes. Serve with a drizzle of cooked marinade, or good olive oil. Lovely with green salad and coleslaw.

SQUID, CHILLI & LEMON SALAD

Serves 2

- 1 chilli
- Juice of 1 lemon
- 1 squid, cleaned (ask your fishmonger to do this)
- 1 tbsp olive oil
- 2 mint sprigs, leaves picked
- 2 handfuls mixed salad leaves

1 Finely dice the chilli and combine with the lemon juice in a bowl. Set aside while you prepare the squid.
2 Separate the tentacles, slice them in half, and cut the rest into bite size pieces. Place the squid in the lemon and chilli mixture, cover, and set aside to marinate for 30-60 minutes.
3 Once the squid is marinated, heat the oil in a frying pan over a medium heat and cook the squid for a few minutes on each side. (Be careful, as it may spit a little when you add it to the pan.) Toss with the mint leaves and salad leaves.

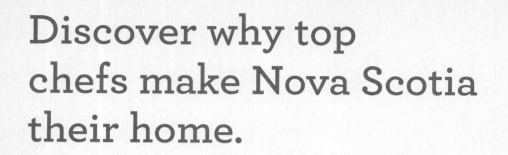

Discover why top chefs make Nova Scotia their home.

Let's start with what's obvious to all who have visited us – Nova Scotia is beautiful. Chefs are artists, and like all true artists, they're not only inspired by their chosen medium – but by the places that surround them.

Perched on Canada's Atlantic Coast, Nova Scotia is renowned as a destination that stirs all the senses. From the Cabot Trail – named the most scenic drive in North America – to the endless white sandy coves, there is no end of treasure here. Our shoreline is peppered with vibrant villages and historical attractions. Majestic natural wonders like the world's highest tides in the Bay of Fundy, give way to gentler surf that sculpts our warm quiet beaches.

Given this impressive backdrop, it's telling that our cuisine is able to take centre stage so effortlessly. It all comes down to ingredients. Here you'll encounter a culinary paradise where local food isn't a movement; it's a way of life. Experience fresh, succulent seafood, mouthwatering produce from our traditional valley farms, and acclaimed wine from our vintners.

Come discover a pantry of inspiration surrounded by a feast for all your senses.

NOVA SCOTIA.COM   Freephone 00800 1565 0000

Wild Caraway Seafood Chowder

Serves 12

200g bacon – small dice
4 lg onions – medium dice
15 cloves of garlic – crushed
8 stalks of celery – medium dice
6-8 med carrots – medium dice
kernels from 8 ears of fresh corn
10 lg potatoes – 1cm dice

*Sweat all ingredients above except
potatoes in a large wide pot using the
fat from the bacon as oil, season with
salt and pepper, continue until the veg is
starting to soften, then add the potatoes.*

3-4 ltr's fish stock to cover
1 ltr single cream

*Cover the potato-veg mix with fish stock,
add bay leaves and bring to the boil
stirring occasionally, when the boiling
point is reached turn off the heat and
add the cream.*

1lb butter
1lb haddock
1lb flounder
1lb halibut
1lb charr
1lb small scallops

*In a large/wide frying pan melt 1/5 of
the butter when it starts to foam add the
diced haddock and poach in the butter
until the outside is white and set, remove
from the pan and repeat with remaining
butter and seafood until all the seafood
is cooked.*

Finishing herbs
Tarragon, Parsley, Chives, Dill

*Return the chowder to the heat and add
all the seafood and chopped fresh herbs,
check for seasoning and serve.*

*The base of the chowder may be made a
day in advance, simply omit the cream,
seafood and herbs until you wish to serve
it. It may also be frozen at this stage
although the potatoes and vegetables
tend to break up when it is reheated but
it will still taste great!*

SMOKED SALMON TOASTS

MONKFISH KEBABS

SMOKED SALMON TOASTS
Recipe by Union Jacks
Serves 6-8

- 1 avocado, halved, stone removed, flesh scooped out
- 1 tbsp crème fraîche
- 1 lemon, plus wedges to serve
- 70g radishes, sliced
- 3 dill sprigs, fronds picked and chopped
- 1 tbsp cider vinegar
- 12-16 slices of crispbread or thinly sliced and toasted rye bread
- 200g smoked salmon
- ½ punnet salad cress
- A handful of red vein sorrel or other colourful baby leaves
- Rapeseed oil

1 Mash the avocado flesh with the crème fraîche until completely smooth. If you're worried about it discolouring, add a small squeeze of lemon juice. Season with a little salt and ground black pepper, if you like. Toss the radish slices with the dill, vinegar and a little pinch of salt.
2 Spread the avocado over the slices of crispbread or rye toast, then top with slices of salmon. Sprinkle over the radish slices, then finish with a scattering of the salad cress and leaves, and a drizzle of rapeseed oil. Serve with the lemon wedges on the side.

MONKFISH KEBABS
Recipe by Fifteen London
Makes 8 kebabs

- 16 slices of pancetta
- 600g monkfish tail cut into 16 cubes
- About 200g day-old focaccia, cut into 16 cubes, sprinkled with water
- 8 wooden skewers or long sticks of rosemary, leaves stripped
- 8 long red chillies, cut into halves
- 2 lemons, cut into wedges, plus juice of 1 to serve
- 2 red onions, each cut in 8 wedges
- Olive oil

1 Wrap the pancetta around 8 pieces of the monkfish and 8 pieces of the focaccia, and set aside with the rest of kebab ingredients.
2 Starting with the stalk half of each chilli, build the kebabs by threading the ingredients onto the skewers. Be as creative as you like, although ideally each kebab will have the same quantities of bread, onion, chillies and lemon. Brush the kebabs with a little of the olive oil.
3 Heat the barbecue to full whack, then grill the kebabs for 8-10 minutes, until the fish is cooked through. Keep moving them around. (The fish may need up to 10 minutes in a 180C/gas 4 oven to ensure it's cooked through after the pancetta is crisp.) Squeeze over the lemon juice and serve.

GRILLED SMOKIES
Lovage is a herb with a flavour like celery and parsley. This recipe uses simple ingredients, and is a brilliant way to have smoked fish in summer.
Serves 4

- 125g butter, softened
- A bunch of lovage or sorrel, finely chopped
- ¼ whole nutmeg, finely grated
- Grated zest of ½ lemon
- 4 Arbroath smokies

1 Mix the softened butter with the lovage or sorrel, nutmeg, zest and a pinch of salt. Wrap the butter in a piece of greaseproof paper, roll into a sausage shape, and twist the ends of the paper to seal. Pop in the fridge until needed. It will last for at least 1-2 weeks in the fridge.
2 Preheat your grill to high. Carefully remove the string from the smokies, split each one along one side with a sharp knife, then flatten out and remove the large bone. Wet a large piece of greaseproof paper, scrunch it up and place on a baking tray, still scrunched up. Place the smokies on top, skin-side up, and cook under the grill for 3 minutes, then very carefully turn them over and pop a couple of knobs of the butter on each one. Pop back under the grill for 3 more minutes, until hot. Serve with lemon wedges and fresh bread.

GRILLED SMOKIES

GINGER & HONEY CHICKEN WINGS

GINGER & HONEY CHICKEN WINGS

Chicken wings are tasty, cheap and great flavour carriers. Marinate overnight for the best flavour and bring the wings to room temperature before barbecuing.

Serves 6-8

- 25 chicken wings

Ginger & honey marinade

- 5 spring onions, finely sliced
- 5 tbsp honey
- 2 tbsp soy sauce
- 1 red chilli, sliced
- 1-2 cm ginger, grated
- 4-5 thyme sprigs, leaves picked

1 Mix all the marinade ingredients in a bowl to make a sticky sauce.
2 Place the chicken wings in a single layer in a wide, shallow, nonreactive dish. Pour the marinade over the chicken, cover with clingfilm and place in the fridge to marinate for 24 hours.
3 Heat your barbecue or griddle pan until nice and hot. Cook the wings for 15-20 minutes, turning often, until dark and the juices run clear when the chicken is pierced with a skewer. If cooking on a griddle, finish the wings in the oven at 180C/gas 4 for 10-15 minutes to ensure they're cooked through.

BOMBAY STREET-FOOD SALAD

Serves 4

- A thumb-sized piece of ginger, roughly chopped
- 2 tsp garam masala
- 3 garlic cloves
- 1 red chilli, halved lengthways
- 1 tsp cumin seeds
- 1 tsp turmeric
- A large bunch of coriander, roughly chopped
- 2-3 tbsp fat-free plain yoghurt
- Juice of 1 lemon
- 2 skinless chicken breasts, sliced into 1-2cm strips
- 2 baking potatoes, cut into chunks
- 2 soft round lettuces, leaves rinsed and spun dry
- 1 tbsp tamarind paste
- 1 tbsp agave syrup or honey
- Groundnut oil
- ½ tsp mustard seeds
- 150g mixed sprouts
- 1½ red onions, finely chopped
- 2 ripe tomatoes, deseeded and chopped
- 2 poppadoms

1 Blitz the ginger, garam masala, 2 garlic cloves, chilli, half the cumin seeds and turmeric, most of the coriander, yoghurt and lemon juice in a blender to get a creamy paste. Spoon into a large bowl, add the chicken and mix well. Cover with clingfilm and marinate in the fridge for at least 30 minutes, preferably a few hours.
2 Meanwhile, cook the potatoes in a pan of salted boiling water until just cooked through. Drain and steam dry.
3 Arrange the lettuce leaves on a tray, like cups. Mix the tamarind paste, agave or honey and a pinch of salt in a bowl with a splash of water, then set aside.
4 Heat a drizzle of groundnut oil in a large nonstick pan over a medium heat. Finely slice the remaining garlic and add to the pan. Fry until lightly golden, then add the remaining cumin seeds and turmeric, mustard seeds and mixed sprouts. Fry for 10-15 minutes, until really golden and crisp, keeping things moving. Stir through the cooked potato and onion, just to coat, then place in a bowl till needed. Wipe out the pan and place back over a medium-high heat.
5 Remove the chicken from the fridge and thread it between 4 metal or pre-soaked bamboo skewers (be sure you don't pack them too tightly). Drizzle a little oil into the pan and fry the chicken for 4-6 minutes each side, or until golden and cooked through.
6 Mix the tomatoes and fried potatoes and divide between the lettuce cups. Top with the remaining coriander, crushed poppadoms and serve with the chicken and a drizzle of dressing.

BOMBAY STREET-FOOD SALAD

PORK BELLY & WATERMELON SALAD

LAMB LEG STEAKS

PORK BELLY & WATERMELON SALAD

"Inspired by one of my favourite things on the menu at Fatty Crab in New York, the flavours here are a knockout," says Jamie. You can roast the pork the day before you serve it, if you like. It's also great with sticky rice.

Serves 6

- A thumb-sized piece of ginger, finely grated
- 2 tsp sichuan pepper
- 1 tsp allspice
- 1kg pork belly
- Olive oil
- 3 tbsp runny honey
- 1 tbsp soy sauce
- 2 tbsp sesame seeds
- 1 small watermelon, cut into chunky, thumb-sized pieces
- ½ bunch of coriander, leaves picked
- ½ bunch of spring onions, sliced

Ginger dressing

- 25g pickled ginger
- 1 lime
- 1 tbsp fish sauce
- 1 tbsp soy sauce
- 1 red chilli, finely chopped

1 Preheat the oven to 160C/gas 2½. Rub the ginger, sichuan pepper, allspice and a pinch of salt into the pork. Place the meat in a roasting tray along with a splash of water, cover with tin foil and roast for 2½–3 hours, or until cooked and easy to pull apart.
2 Let the pork cool, then cut into chunky, thumb-sized lardons. Heat a little olive oil in a large frying pan over a medium-high heat, add the lardons and cook for 2-3 minutes, or until golden on each side. In the last 30 seconds, drizzle with the honey, soy and sesame seeds.
3 For the ginger dressing, shake all the ingredients together in a clean jam jar.
4 Toss the pork with the watermelon and the dressing on a platter. Serve scattered with the coriander leaves and sliced spring onion.

LAMB LEG STEAKS

Recipe by Fifteen London
Serves 4

- 2 x 300-400g lamb leg steaks
- 120ml olive oil
- 1 smoked garlic bulb
- A bunch of rosemary, tied together with string to form a brush
- Zest of 1 lemon
- 200ml plain yoghurt

Lemon & rosemary marinade

- 2 garlic cloves, crushed
- Grated zest of 1 lemon
- A few glugs of olive oil
- A few sprigs of rosemary

1 For the marinade, combine all the ingredients in a wide bowl. Place the lamb leg steaks in the marinade, turn to coat, cover with clingfilm and leave in the fridge to marinate for at least 2 hours.
2 When you're ready to cook, pour the olive oil into a small stainless steel pot. Smash the garlic bulb with a pestle and mortar and add to the oil. Sit the rosemary brush in the pot and leave on the side of the barbecue to warm up and infuse the lovely flavours.
3 Heat your barbecue to a high heat then turn down to moderate. Remove the lamb from the marinade, season, and place on the barbecue. Cook to your taste: about 8 minutes for rare, 10 for medium, 14 for well done, brushing occasionally with olive oil using the rosemary brush (you may not need to use all the oil).Remove the steaks from the heat, cover with tin foil, and leave to rest for a few minutes. To serve, grate the lemon zest into the yoghurt, then spoon it over the lamb.

BRUNCH SALAD

BRUNCH SALAD
Serves 4

- Olive oil
- 2 sweetcorn cobs
- 2 ripe avocados, flesh quartered
- 4 rashers of smoked streaky bacon
- 2 baby gem lettuces, cut into thin wedges
- 100g baby spinach
- 30g tortilla chips, crunched up
- 20g cress (optional)

Yoghurt dressing
- 2 tbsp fat-free plain yoghurt
- A few flat-leaf parsley sprigs, leaves picked and chopped
- Juice of ½ lemon
- Extra-virgin olive oil

1 Put a griddle pan over a high heat. Once it's hot, pour in a little oil, then add your corn cobs; when you hear them pop and crackle, start turning them till they're cooked all the way round. A few minutes before they're ready, add the avocado and cook – don't move it– till charred. Remove both, then griddle the bacon till crisp.
2 When the corn has cooled a little, run a sharp knife down the sides to slice off the kernels, keeping them in chunks, like beehives, if you like.
3 For the dressing, add the ingredients to a clean jar. Add enough oil to get a consistency you like. Put the lid on and shake to combine, then season to taste.
4 Pile the lettuce, spinach, corn and avocado on a platter and pour over half the dressing. Scatter with the tortilla chips, crumble over the bacon, drizzle on the rest of the dressing and snip over some cress, if you fancy.

LA-STYLE TURKEY SALAD

"Turkey often only gets a look in at Christmas, but it's a good source of lean protein that's generally available all year round," says Jamie. "Paired with avocado, it makes for a cracking salad. I've called it LA-style because it melds Mexican flavours and fresh produce in a very Californian way."
Serves 4–6

- ½ tsp cayenne pepper
- 1 tbsp paprika
- ½ tsp white pepper
- 1 tsp dried oregano
- Extra-virgin olive oil
- 2 skinless turkey breasts, or about 600g chicken if you prefer
- 2 corn tortillas, sliced into 1cm strips
- 4 rashers of smoked streaky bacon
- 1 cos lettuce, cut into wedges
- 1 little gem lettuce, cut into wedges
- 1–2 pink or red grapefruit, peeled and segmented
- Mixed baby cress, to serve (optional)

Avocado dressing
- 2 ripe avocados, halved and stoned
- 4 tbsp fat-free plain yoghurt
- 2 limes, plus extra to serve
- 1 jalapeno or red chilli
- A large bunch of coriander

1 Preheat your oven to 180C/gas 4. Place a griddle pan over a high heat. Mix the cayenne pepper, paprika, white pepper and oregano with a good pinch of salt and a little olive oil and rub all over the turkey breast. Put the turkey on the pan, turn the heat to medium, and cook for 20–25 minutes, turning halfway.
2 Meanwhile, make the dressing. Blitz 1 avocado in a blender with the yoghurt, lime juice, jalapeno, most of the coriander and a good drizzle of olive oil until you have a creamy dressing. Season to taste, add a splash of water to loosen, if needed, then set aside.
3 Spread the corn tortilla strips over a baking sheet and bake in the oven for a few minutes, until golden and crisp.
4 When your turkey is almost cooked, add the bacon to the pan for the last few minutes to crisp up. Once done, transfer the turkey to a board to rest, then thinly slice. Crudely toss the turkey in a bowl with the lettuce wedges and avocado dressing, then scatter over a board. Crumble over the bacon, add the tortilla strips, then use a spoon to scoop out little nuggets of the remaining avocado and add these. Finish with grapefruit segments, mixed cress, if using, and the remaining coriander leaves. Serve with limes for squeezing over.

EPIC SALAD

LA-STYLE TURKEY SALAD

STRAWBERRY MESS

STRAWBERRY MESS

"Sweet, juicy strawberries are one of my favourite fruits," says Jamie. "I wanted to recreate the famous Eton mess, but instead of it being the usual muddled mix, I wanted a proper pudding with some structure – which I then dropped from a height."

Serves 10

- 6 egg whites
- 300g golden caster sugar, plus 1-2 tbsp extra, depending on the sweetness of the strawberries
- 500g strawberries, hulled, larger ones halved
- 400ml double cream
- 1 vanilla pod, split lengthways and seeds scraped out
- 2 tbsp icing sugar, sifted

1 Preheat the oven to 150C/gas 2 and line a 40cm x 25cm baking tray with a sheet of baking paper. Put your egg whites in a bowl and whisk with an electric hand whisk or stand mixer on medium speed until firm peaks form. With the mixer still running, gradually add the sugar and a pinch of salt. Turn the mixer up to its highest setting and continue to whisk for 6–7 minutes, until the meringue is white and glossy. Pinch some between your fingers. If it's completely smooth, it's ready; if it's slightly granular, keep whisking.
2 Dot each corner of the baking paper with a small blob of meringue, then turn it over and use the meringue to stick the paper to the tray. Spoon the rest of the meringue onto the paper and, using the back of your spoon, swirl it into a large oval shape. Bake in the oven for 1 hour, or until crisp on the outside and a little soft on the inside. Remove the meringue from the oven and let it cool completely, then transfer to a nice board or platter.
3 Place the strawberries in a bowl with the extra sugar and leave for 15 minutes. Meanwhile, whip the cream with the vanilla seeds and icing sugar until it forms soft peaks.
4 With clean hands, scrunch some of the strawberries so you have a mix of pulp and pieces. To assemble the strawberry mess, drop the meringue onto the board so it breaks up, then top with the cream and strawberries. Serve immediately.

CELERY WITH GINGER & STRAWBERRIES

CELERY WITH GINGER & STRAWBERRIES

This bright salad is brilliant, unusual and wonderfully refreshing.

Serves 2

- 2 celery hearts
- 3cm piece of ginger, peeled
- 75g sugar
- 200g ripe strawberries, sliced
- 2 small lumps of crystallised ginger

1 Remove the outer celery stalks and trim the base of the hearts with a sharp knife, keeping the heart in 1 piece. Trim the celery heart to about 10cm long.
2 Place the celery on a chopping board and, with a sharp knife, carve long thin strips, at a slanting angle.
3 Thinly slice the ginger into 5 or 6 pieces, then place in a small pan with the sugar and 150ml water. Place the pan over a medium heat and bring to the boil. Reduce the heat to a simmer for 10 minutes, then turn off.
4 Take a serving plate and scatter over an even layer of celery slices. Cover with a layer of sliced strawberries, then one more layer of each, making sure the top layer has some pretty strawberry slices in it. Spoon the syrup over the top – leaving the ginger in the pan – ensuring you coat all the celery and strawberries.
5 Leave everything to macerate for 10 minutes, then slice the crystallised ginger really thinly and scatter over the top of the salad before serving.

CHERRIES & CHOCOLATE

CHERRIES & CHOCOLATE

There's something about the combination of dark chocolate and cherries that just seems to work.

Serves 6

- 500g cherries, stoned
- 150g dark 70% cocoa chocolate, broken into pieces
- 2 star anise
- 1½ tbsp runny honey
- 75ml chianti or other fruity red wine
- Single cream (optional), to serve

1 Leave the cherries in the fridge until they're nice and cold. (You can serve them at room temperature, but they're much nicer chilled for this recipe.)
2 Place the chocolate and star anise in a heatproof bowl and warm over a pan of gently simmering water, making sure the water doesn't touch the bowl. Once all of the chocolate has melted, stir in the honey and red wine.
3 Pour the chocolate sauce into a bowl

(discard the star anise), swirl in a little cream if you fancy it, and serve alongside the chilled cherries, letting everyone help themselves.

....

ULTIMATE VICTORIA SANDWICH SPONGE

This classic cake is, of course, named after Queen Victoria, the only monarch to reign longer than the current Queen. It's relatively easy to make but does have a few quirks: you need to get as much air into it as possible, and be mindful of its sensitivity to variations in heat. Know your oven well and invest in an oven thermometer!

Serves 14

- 225g unsalted butter, cubed and softened, plus extra to grease
- 225g white caster sugar
- 1 tsp vanilla extract
- 4 eggs, beaten
- 225g self-raising flour, sifted
- 1 tsp baking powder

- ¼ tsp salt
- A splash of milk

Filling

- 250g fresh strawberries, hulled and roughly sliced
- 200ml double cream
- 1 vanilla pod, seeds scraped
- 1½ tbsp icing sugar

1 Preheat the oven to 180C/gas 4. Grease 2 round 20cm sandwich tins and line the bases. Cream the butter and sugar together in a large mixing bowl until pale and fluffy. Mix in the vanilla extract.
2 Gradually mix the beaten eggs into the creamed butter and sugar. Fold in the flour, baking powder and salt with a large metal spoon until just incorporated (don't overmix).
3 Stir in a splash of milk to loosen the batter, then evenly divide it between the 2 cake tins. Bake the cakes in the oven for 22-25 minutes, until golden and cooked through. (To test, insert a skewer into the middle of a cake; it's ready when the skewer comes out clean.) Leave to cool in the tins for 5 minutes, then turn onto a wire rack to cool completely. Once completely cool, sandwich with your choice of filling or use our suggestion. (Jam is the traditional choice, but lemon curd is nice, too; whipped cream is optional, but some prefer buttercream).
4 Pour the cream into a large bowl, scrape in the vanilla seeds and whisk until you have soft peaks. Sift in the icing sugar and gently fold through. Place one of the cakes on your chosen plate or cake stand and spread over the vanilla cream, but not right to the edges or it will spill later. Scatter the strawberries and top with the second cake. Dust with icing sugar and top with extra strawberries.

ENGLISH CLASSIC

COOL &
EASY

LIMONCELLO & FRUIT SALAD FRO-YO

POACHED PEACHES

SUMMER PUDDING

LIMONCELLO & FRUIT SALAD FRO-YO

"If you have any leftover fruit salad, or fruit that's on the turn, chop it and freeze it until you want to make this. Lose the yoghurt if you want to go for more of a sorbet vibe," says Jamie.

Makes about 1.4 litres

- 1kg fruit salad or chopped mixed fruit, fresh or frozen
- 250ml fat-free plain yoghurt
- 2-3 tbsp runny honey, depending on your fruit mix
- 75ml limoncello (optional)
- Ice cream cones, to serve

1 Blitz the fruit salad, yoghurt, honey and limoncello in a food processor until smooth. Taste, and add more honey to sweeten, if needed. Spoon into a freezerproof container and place in the freezer for 1-2 hours, until frozen.
2 Take the fro-yo mixture out of the freezer, pop it back in the processor and blitz again to break up any ice crystals that have formed. When ready to eat, serve scoops in cups or ice cream cones.

POACHED PEACHES

Simple, seasonal, sensational.

Serves 6

- 50g sugar
- 400ml water

- 2 lemongrass stalks, halved lengthways
- 6-8 peaches or 12 apricots, washed

1 Gently heat the sugar and water in a small pan with the lemongrass over a low-medium heat until the sugar has dissolved. Carefully add the peaches or apricots, and gently press a circle of greaseproof paper down on top to keep the fruit covered with liquid. Cook at a very gentle simmer for 4-5 minutes for apricots, or 10-12 minutes for peaches, or till the fruit is tender, but not squishy. Pour into a bowl to cool before serving.

SUMMER PUDDING

It's not traditional to do so, but we like to spread the bread with a little jam to stop it getting too soggy.

Serves 8

- Olive oil, for greasing
- 800g mixed summer berries (raspberries, redcurrants, strawberries, blackcurrants, blackberries), stalks removed, strawberries hulled, quartered
- 150g sugar
- Juice of ½ orange
- ½ tsp vanilla paste (optional)
- 2 tbsp red berry jam
- 7 slices from a large white loaf, crusts removed

1 Grease an 850ml (1.5 pints) pudding basin with a tiny amount of olive oil and then line with 2 sheets of clingfilm, letting a little bit overhang.
2 Place all the berries in a large, heavy-based saucepan with the sugar, orange juice and vanilla paste (if using). Cook over a low heat for 3-5 minutes, until the sugar dissolves and juices start bleeding from the fruit. Set aside to cool.
3 Spread the jam over the bread. Line the basin with 6 of the slices, with the jam facing inside. Overlap slightly to ensure no gaps, and press the bread against the sides.
4 Spoon the cooled fruit and half its juice into the lined basin, reserving the remaining juice. Cover the pudding with the last slice of bread, then pull over the overhanging clingfilm. Place a saucer that fits inside the basin on top of the pudding, then place a weight, about 2kg, on top of it. Refrigerate overnight to soak up the juices.
5 Strain the leftover juice through a fine sieve into a small pan. Bring to the boil, then simmer for 5-10 minutes, until the juice has reduced into a light syrup. Pour into a jug and keep in the fridge.
6 To serve, open the clingfilm and carefully invert the pudding onto a plate. Slice, drizzle with the syrup and serve with crème fraîche or cream, if you like.

MINT & RASPBERRY JULEP

BERRY & SEED SMOOTHIE

NANNY PAM'S GUINNESS PUNCH

This was created by Pam, the grandmother of our friend chef Lloyd Hayes. She likes to make a batch for Sunday lunches.

Makes 2.2 litres

- 2 x 440ml cans of Guinness
- 397g condensed milk (1 tin)
- 900ml milk
- 1 vanilla pod, split lengthways, seeds scraped (optional)
- A few gratings of nutmeg, to taste
- A pinch of ground cinnamon

1 For the best results, blitz all the ingredients in a blender with a handful of crushed ice, in batches if needed. If you don't have a blender, mix the Guinness, condensed milk and milk in a bowl, and add vanilla seeds (if using) and spices to taste. Serve over ice.

RASPBERRIES Greek myth says that raspberries, once white, were turned red when the nymph Ida pricked her finger while picking the berries for Zeus

MINT & RASPBERRY JULEP

This recipe uses fresh summer raspberries to bring a seasonal twist to a classic cocktail.

Serves 1

- 8 mint leaves
- A small handful of raspberries
- 1 tsp sugar syrup
- Crushed ice
- 50ml bourbon

1 Place the mint, raspberries and sugar syrup in a tumbler and muddle. Set aside to macerate for 10 minutes. Remove the mint and strain the drink into a clean glass. Add a small handful of ice to the glass, then pour over the bourbon. Stir, and finish with more crushed ice.

BERRY & SEED SMOOTHIE

Serves 2

- 400g mixed berries or 100g each of blueberries, raspberries, strawberries and blackberries
- 1 tbsp mixed hemp seeds, linseeds or flaxseeds, or 1 tsp of each
- 1 banana, peeled
- Juice of 2 oranges

1 Blitz everything in a blender, preferably straight from the fridge (or blend with a few ice cubes). Serve immediately. This is the breakfast of champions.

STRAWBERRY & COCONUT SMOOTHIE

Not pictured
Serves 2

- 350g strawberries, hulled
- 200ml coconut water
- 1 mint sprig, leaves picked
- Ice, to serve

1 Blitz together all the ingredients in a blender or in a jug using a stick blender. Put some ice in 2 glasses, pour over the smoothie and serve at once.

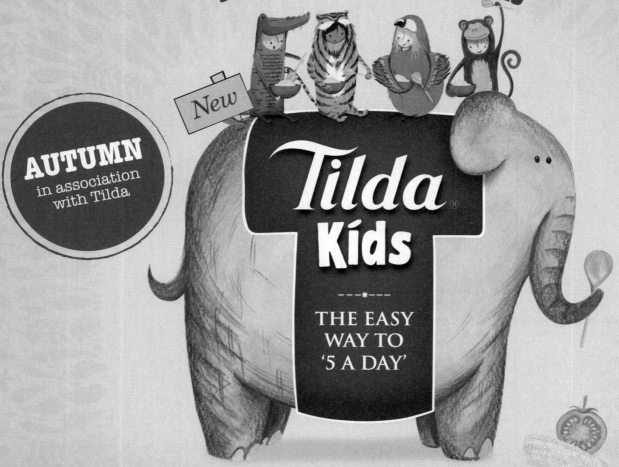

feeding time!

smiley tums... happy mums

AUTUMN in association with Tilda

New

Tilda Kids

THE EASY WAY TO '5 A DAY'

Rice & veggies, full of goodness and tastes great too!

Yummy with everything!

Find us in the rice aisle and at *tilda.com*

AUTUMN

Let's celebrate the harvest of squash, onions, fruit, nuts and brambles with dishes that warm the cockles of the heart

SIMPLE THAI

PORK TOM YUM

PORK TOM YUM

Serves 2

- 2 tsp tom yum paste
- 1 carrot, julienned
- 1 red pepper, julienned
- 150g chestnut mushrooms, finely sliced
- 300g rice noodles
- 100g cooked pork
- ¼ tsp fish sauce
- Juice of ½ lime
- 2 spring onions, sliced, and coriander sprigs, to garnish

1 In a wok or large pan, bring the paste and 500ml water to the boil. Drop in the carrot and pepper, then simmer for 5 minutes. Add the mushrooms, noodles and pork, then simmer for another 5 minutes. Season with the fish sauce and lime juice, ladle into deep bowls and top with spring onions and coriander.

ZUPPA DI VALPELLINE

Cabbage & bread soup with fontina
Serves 8

- 800g–1kg savoy cabbage, cavolo nero or a mixture
- 2.5 litres vegetable stock
- Olive oil
- A few sage sprigs, leaves picked
- 4 garlic cloves, finely sliced
- 2 onions, finely sliced
- 4 anchovy fillets, in oil
- 1 large loaf of Italian country-style bread, such as pugliese
- 200g fontina, coarsely grated

1 Remove the leaves from the cabbage and cavolo nero, cut off the stems and rinse the leaves well. Roll them up like large cigars and cut into 5mm slices.
2 Bring the vegetable stock to the boil in a large saucepan. Blanch the shredded cabbage in the stock for 5 minutes, then remove to a bowl with a slotted spoon and set aside till needed. Keep the vegetable stock hot in the pan.

3 Preheat the oven to 180C/gas 4. Heat a good glug of olive oil in a nonstick frying pan. Shred most of the sage leaves (leave a few whole for garnishing) and add to the pan along with the garlic. Fry over a medium heat for a couple of minutes, until the garlic is golden. Add the onion and anchovies and lower the heat. Sauté for 10–15 minutes, until the onion is soft and sticky but not coloured, and the anchovies have broken down. Add the reserved cabbage to the pan, season well and mix everything together. Remove from the heat.
4 Cut the bread into 12–15 slices and toast all but 5 of them until golden. Get a wide, deep ovenproof dish (about 25cm across) and start layering up the soup. Start with half of the toast, cutting the slices if necessary to create a secure, even layer on the bottom. Top with half of the cabbage and onion mixture, and sprinkle over a third of the grated cheese. Layer with the remaining toast, cabbage and a third more cheese. Ladle over the stock, until the dish is almost full, then finish with a layer of the untoasted bread. Push and submerge the bread, and drizzle with olive oil. Scatter over the remaining cheese and sage leaves, and cover the dish with foil. Bake in the oven for 20 minutes, then remove the foil and bake for a further 15 minutes, until the soup is golden and bubbling up. Serve immediately.

ZUPPA DI VALPELLINE

ENGLISH ONION SOUP

ENGLISH ONION SOUP

A French classic is given a local twist with cheddar, cider and hot mustard.
Serves 4

- 20g butter
- 4 onions, sliced
- 2 garlic cloves, chopped
- 300ml Somerset cider
- 1 litre chicken stock
- 8 slices of baguette
- 75g cheddar
- 1 tsp English mustard
- 1 egg
- 1 tbsp chives

1 Melt the butter in a pan and gently cook the onions for 40 minutes, until they start to turn golden. Add the garlic for the last few minutes. Pour over the cider and let it bubble away until reduced by half. Add the stock, bring to the boil and cook for 10 minutes.
2 Preheat the grill to full whack and place the bread on a baking tray. Toast the bread lightly on each side. Meanwhile, in a bowl, mix the cheddar, mustard, egg and half the chives. Remove the bread from the oven and divide the cheddar mix between the toasts. Pop the tray back under the grill till the topping is golden. Ladle the soup into bowls and serve with half the toasts on the side and half on top, sprinkled with the remaining chives.

WHITE GAZPACHO WITH CHORIZO

Most people think of gazpacho as being red, made with tomatoes and peppers, but this is another way the Spanish like to make cold soup.
Serves 4

- 6 slices of rustic bread, crusts removed
- 100g blanched, unsalted marcona almonds (see note)
- 2 large garlic cloves
- 100g white seedless grapes
- 3 tbsp sherry vinegar
- 100ml extra-virgin olive oil
- 1 tbsp olive oil
- A pinch of cayenne pepper
- 2 tbsp flaked almonds
- 80g chorizo, finely sliced
- 2 tbsp chopped flat-leaf parsley

1 Preheat the oven to 180C/gas 4. Lightly toast the bread, then arrange it in a single layer in a snug-fitting baking tray and pour over 250ml of ice-cold water. Set aside to soften.
2 Heat a frying pan and toast the marcona almonds over a low heat for 5 minutes until golden. Pop into a food processor with the garlic and pulse until finely ground. Add the bread and grapes and blend until smooth.
3 Transfer the mixture to a bowl and whisk in the vinegar, followed by the olive oil and 500ml of ice-cold water. Strain through a fine sieve, season with cayenne pepper and salt, then chill in the fridge until ready to eat.
4 When almost ready to serve, toast the flaked almonds in a hot pan, then remove. Add the chorizo slices and fry until crisp. Reserve the oil.
5 Serve the soup in chilled bowls topped with chorizo, flaked almonds, parsley and a drizzle of the chorizo oil.
Note If you can't find marcona almonds at your supermarket, find them online at melburyandappleton.co.uk, or you can substitute regular blanched almonds.

WHITE GAZPACHO WITH CHORIZO & ALMONDS

The rice for all occasions

Three delicious recipes for autumn – just add Tilda to taste

Chicken and Almond Pilaf

Preparation time: 10 minutes
Cooking time: 1 hour | *Serves 4*

Ingredients:
240g Tilda Wholegrain Basmati rice
2 tbsp veg oil
8 chicken drumsticks, skinned and scored (approx. 1kg)
2cm piece fresh ginger, chopped
2 cloves garlic, chopped
2 tsp cumin seeds, lightly crushed
2 tsp coriander seeds, lightly crushed
1 tsp fenugreek
1 tsp black mustard seeds
2-3 cloves
50g flaked almonds
600ml chicken stock
200g green beans, halved

Preparation:
Preheat the oven to 200oC, gas mark 6.
Heat the oil in a frying pan and fry the chicken for 4-5 minutes until golden. Add the ginger, garlic and dry spices and cook for a further minute. Transfer to a casserole dish and stir in the remaining ingredients.
Cover and cook for 1 hour until the rice is tender and chicken is cooked through.
Season to taste before serving.

Cooking Tips:
Try using Tilda Basmati & Wild rice instead of the Wholegrain rice, as the unique appearance and taste of the wild rice brings a touch of the exotic to the dish

Sweetcorn, Broccoli and Cheese Mini Frittatas

Preparation time: 10 minutes
Cooking time: 15 minutes
Makes 24 Frittatas

Ingredients
1 pouch Tilda Kids Sunshine Vegetable Rice
1 small onion, finely chopped, about 50g
50g, cooked broccoli, cut into small pieces
4 tbsps canned sweetcorn, drained
100g grated cheddar cheese
4 eggs, beaten
A few snipped chives
Salt & pepper

Preparation
Pre-heat the oven to 200°c, 180°c fan or Gas Mark 6. Empty contents of one pouch of Tilda Kids Sunshine Vegetable Rice into a large jug and stir in the onion, cooked broccoli, sweetcorn, cheese and chives. In a separate bowl beat the eggs together. Add the eggs to the rice mix and season well. Grease a non-stick 12 hole mini muffin tin. Use half the mix and divide between the 12 holes. Cook in the oven for 15 minutes and then cook another batch.

Seafood and Chilli Rice Gumbo

Preparation time: 5 minutes
Cooking time: 10 minutes
Serves 2-3

Ingredients:
250g pack Tilda Mexican Chilli & Bean Steamed Basmati rice
400g can chopped tomatoes
½ tsp smoked paprika
1 clove garlic, chopped
1 green pepper, diced
300g cod fillet, cubed
150g cooked peeled tiger prawns
75g cooked mussels
2 tbsp chopped parsley

Preparation:
Place the tomatoes, paprika, garlic and pepper into a large frying pan and bring to the boil, add the fish and seafood. Simmer for 5-7 minutes until slightly thickened.
Stir in the rice straight from the pack, and cook for 2 minutes, stirring occasionally. Stir in the parsley and then serve

Cooking Tips:
Try using a pack of prepared seafood mix. This is just as delicious and slightly sweeter if you use Tilda Sweet Chilli and Lime variety.

Tilda
Legendary Rice

Spicy Cauliflower with Coconut Rice

Preparation time: 15 minutes
Cooking time: 20 minutes | Serves 4

Ingredients:
240g Tilda Pure Basmati rice
400ml can coconut milk
300ml vegetable stock
1 cauliflower, cut into small florets, approx. 370g
1 tbsp oil
1 onion, sliced (170g)
½–1 tsp red chilli flakes
1 tbsp medium curry powder
2 tsp black mustard seeds
150g frozen peas
50ml water
50g toasted flaked almonds (optional)
50g sultanas
20g pack coriander, chopped

Preparation:
Boil the rice with the coconut milk and stock for 15–20 minutes, uncovered, stirring occasionally. Meanwhile, in another pan cook the cauliflower in boiling water for 5 minutes, drain. Heat the oil in a frying pan and fry 1 tsp mustard seeds, until they pop, add the onion and chilli flakes and continue to fry for 3–4 minutes. Add the curry powder, cauliflower, peas and 50ml water and fry for 2–3 minutes. Season to taste. Stir the almonds, sultanas, coriander and remaining mustard seeds into the rice, and serve with the spicy cauliflower.

Cooking Tips:
For a quick alternative, use 2 x 250g packs Tilda Coconut, Chilli & Lemongrass rice and then stir in the almonds, sultanas and coriander.

ROASTED SQUASH & COUSCOUS SALAD

ROASTED SQUASH & COUSCOUS SALAD
Serves 4 as a side
- 1 butternut squash, peeled
- 1 green chilli, finely chopped
- 1 tbsp cumin seeds
- 5 thyme sprigs
- 3 tbsp olive oil
- 100g couscous
- Zest and juice of ½ lemon
- 2 tbsp pumpkin seeds, toasted

1 Preheat the oven to 190C/gas 5. Chop the butternut squash into large chunks and place in a roasting dish with the chilli. Scatter over the cumin seeds and thyme. Toss together with 2 tablespoons of the olive oil. Season with a pinch of sea salt and roast for 45–50 minutes, until cooked and lightly golden, turning halfway through.
2 Place the couscous in a bowl and pour over enough boiling water to sit 1cm above the couscous. Cover the bowl and leave for 10 minutes. Uncover and fluff with a fork, stir in the lemon zest, juice, the squash and the remaining olive oil. Serve scattered with the pumpkin seeds.

SWEET POTATO, CHICKPEA & SPINACH CURRY

Moroccan Baked Lamb with Saffron Rice

Preparation time: 15 minutes
Cooking time: 1 hour | Serves 4

Ingredients:
240g Tilda Pure Basmati rice
600g diced leg of lamb
1 tbsp harissa (25g)
1 tsp ground cumin
Zest and juice of 1 lemon
1 tbsp oil
50g pitted black olives, sliced
400g can chickpeas, drained
Pinch saffron
600ml hot lamb stock

Preparation:
Preheat the oven to 200°C, gas mark 6. Mix the lamb with the harissa, cumin and lemon zest and marinate for 10 minutes. Heat the oil in a large frying pan and fry the lamb for 3-4 minutes. Stir in the lemon juice and olives. Meanwhile, place the rice, chickpeas and saffron in a Moroccan tagine or casserole dish and pour over the stock. Top with the lamb mixture, cover and bake for 1 hour or until the liquid is absorbed and the lamb is tender.

Cooking Tips:
For a vegetarian option, replace the lamb and fry 1 chopped onion in oil with the harissa and add 1 diced aubergine and 500g diced butternut squash and replace the lamb stock for vegetable stock.

For more inspirational recipes, visit tilda.com

SWEET POTATO, CHICKPEA & SPINACH CURRY

Serves 6

- 2 tbsp olive oil
- 2 red onions, sliced
- 3 tbsp rogan josh paste
- 1 red chilli, finely chopped
- 3cm piece of ginger, grated
- A bunch of coriander, stalks chopped, leaves picked
- 3 sweet potatoes, cut into 2cm chunks
- 1 x 400g tin chickpeas, drained
- 8 ripe tomatoes, roughly chopped or 1 x 400g tin chopped tomatoes
- 1 x 400ml tin light coconut milk
- 400g spinach, washed
- Poppadoms and rice, to serve

1 Heat the olive oil in a large saucepan over a medium heat. Add the onion and the curry paste, mix well, then cook for 10 minutes, stirring occasionally, until the onion is soft and golden.
2 Add the chilli, ginger, coriander stalks, sweet potato and tinned chickpeas. Cook for 5 minutes. Add the tinned tomatoes and 200ml water and bring to the boil. Reduce the heat to a simmer, then cover and cook for 10-15 minutes. Remove the lid, then cook for a further 15-20 minutes, stirring occasionally, until the sweet potato is cooked through and the sauce has thickened. Stir in the coconut milk and cook for a couple of minutes, then stir in the spinach and continue to cook until it has just wilted. Scatter over the coriander leaves, then serve with poppadums and rice.
3 To freeze the curry for another time, leave to cool in the pan, then spoon into portion-sized containers or freezer bags and freeze. The curry will keep in the freezer for up to 3 months.

SAMBHARO

ROAST ONION SALAD WITH BLUE CHEESE DRESSING
Serves 4

- 4 red onions, skins on
- 8 slices of ciabatta or baguette
- Red wine vinegar
- Extra-virgin olive oil
- 2 cox's apples, coarsely grated
- 1 red chilli, coarsely grated
- A handful of shelled walnuts, finely sliced or shaved on a mandolin
- Juice of ½ lemon
- 2 handfuls of salad leaves, such as purslane, watercress, rocket
- 4–6 rashers of pancetta
- Chive flowers (optional)

Blue cheese dressing
- 2 spring onions, chopped
- 2 tbsp fat-free plain yoghurt
- 50g roquefort cheese
- ½ bunch of chives, chopped

1 Preheat the oven to 170C/gas 3. Trim the roots and tops from the onions but leave the skins on. Put the ciabatta or baguette in a small ovenproof dish and drizzle over a tiny amount of olive oil. Sit the onions on top, drizzle with vinegar and cook for 60–75 minutes, till quite soft. Check halfway through and move around a bit so the bread doesn't dry out.
2 Meanwhile, combine the apple, chilli and walnuts in a large bowl. Season with salt and pepper, and dress with lemon juice and olive oil.
3 For the blue cheese dressing, blitz all the ingredients in a blender with a drizzle of olive oil and a splash of water to loosen, if needed. Season to taste, then set aside until needed.
4 Once the onions start feeling soft in the middle, drape the pancetta around them and return the dish to the oven for 20 minutes, or until the pancetta is golden and crisp and the onions are sweet and sticky.
5 To serve, toss the salad leaves and blue cheese dressing with the apple, chilli and walnuts and spread over a platter. Squeeze the onions from their skins onto the toasts, then crumble over the crispy pancetta. Scatter with chive flowers, if you like, and serve with the onion toasts.

SAMBHARO
Warm cabbage salad
Buy a slightly unripe mango for its tart crunchiness. If you can only find a ripe, sweet mango, omit the sugar.
Serves 4 as a side

- 1 tbsp sunflower oil
- 1 tsp cumin seeds
- ½ tsp mustard seeds
- 1 tsp sesame seeds
- ½ tsp asafoetida
- 120g white cabbage, thinly sliced
- 2 carrots, thinly sliced
- ½ red pepper, thinly sliced
- ½ green pepper, thinly sliced
- ½ firm mango, thinly sliced

- ½ tsp turmeric powder
- ½ tsp red chilli powder
- 1 tsp sugar (optional)
- 1 tbsp lemon juice
- A handful of coriander, leaves picked and chopped, to serve

1 Heat the oil in a wok or deep frying pan over a medium heat, and add the cumin, mustard and sesame seeds, and asafoetida, and fry for few seconds. Stir in the cabbage, carrots, peppers and mango, and stir fry for 2 minutes. Add the turmeric, chilli powder, sugar, lemon juice, and a pinch of salt, and cook for just 1 minute. Sprinkle with coriander.

ROAST ONION SALAD WITH BLUE CHEESE DRESSING

LEEK & PORCINI PAPPARDELLE

AUBERGINE, TOMATO AND GARLIC PASTA

LEEK & PORCINI PAPPARDELLE

Serves 4

- 30g dried porcini mushrooms
- 2 tbsp extra-virgin olive oil
- 2 leeks, cut into thin rounds
- 30g fresh sage leaves, finely chopped
- 4 garlic cloves, crushed or finely chopped
- 50g parmesan, grated
- 150g crème fraîche
- 300g fresh pappardelle

1 Place the mushrooms in a bowl and cover with 250ml boiling water. Leave for 10 minutes to soften. Add the oil to a heavy frying pan, then add the leeks, sage and garlic and gently sauté until soft. Drain the mushrooms, and reserve the liquid. Roughly chop the porcini and add to the pan along with the mushroom liquid. Stir everything well and simmer for 5 minutes. Stir the crème fraîche and parmesan into the pan to form a sauce.
2 Bring a large pan of water to the boil and cook the pappardelle for 2–3 minutes, drain, and pour into the pan with the sauce, mixing thoroughly to coat all of the pasta. Add a splash of cooking water to loosen the sauce if required. Serve with extra parmesan and black pepper, to taste.

AUBERGINE, TOMATO & GARLIC PASTA

Serves 4

- 1 tbsp olive oil
- 1 onion, finely chopped
- 2 garlic cloves, finely chopped
- 1 medium aubergine, cut into 1cm cubes
- ½ tsp smoked paprika
- 5 tomatoes, cut into 1cm cubes
- 400g pasta
- Parmesan, to serve

1 Heat the oil in a large saucepan, add the onion and cook for 5–7 minutes until soft. Add the garlic, aubergine and paprika and cook for 10 minutes. Add the tomatoes, season, and cook for a further 10 minutes until completely softened and the aubergine is cooked through.
2 Meanwhile, bring a large pan of salted water to the boil and cook the pasta according to packet instructions. Toss the sauce through the drained pasta, adding a splash of cooking water to loosen the sauce if required, and serve with plenty of grated parmesan.

SPINACH, BACON & PUMPKIN PASTA

Serves 4-6

- 1 tbsp oil
- 1 onion, sliced
- 1 tsp fennel seeds
- A pinch of dried chilli flakes
- 4 rashers of smoked bacon, chopped
- 1 small pumpkin, peeled and chopped
- 100ml single cream
- A large handful of spinach
- 400g spaghetti pasta
- 2 tbsp pine nuts, toasted, to serve

1 Heat the oil in a pan, add the onion and cook until soft. Add the fennel seeds and chilli flakes, cook for 1 minute, then add the bacon and cook for 5 minutes. Lower the heat, add the pumpkin and cook for 20 minutes, partially covered, until the pumpkin is almost done. Uncover, add the cream and spinach, and cook for 5 minutes.
2 Cook the pasta according to packet instructions, drain, and toss with the sauce. Add a little cooking water, if required. Top with pine nuts to serve.

SPINACH, BACON
& PUMPKIN PASTA

FENNEL, AUBERGINE & CHILLI LASAGNE

MUSHROOMS Autumn is the time to forage for wild mushrooms, and their flavours go perfectly in risottos and pastas as the weather turns cold

MUSHROOM, MASCARPONE & SAGE RISOTTO

FENNEL, AUBERGINE & CHILLI LASAGNE

Serves 4-6

- 2 fennel bulbs, sliced
- 2 aubergines, sliced into 1cm rounds
- 1 tbsp fennel seeds, bashed
- 1 tsp dried chilli
- Olive oil
- 60g butter
- 60g flour
- 600ml milk
- 100g grated parmesan
- 140g lasagne sheets
- 125g mozzarella

1 Preheat the oven to 180C/gas 4. Put the fennel and aubergine in a roasting tray and sprinkle with the fennel seeds, chilli, a little seasoning and a drizzle of oil. Roast for 45-60 minutes, until golden and soft.
2 Melt the butter in a pan over a low heat, add the flour, and stir well for 2 minutes. Slowly whisk in the milk until you have a smooth sauce. Simmer for 3 minutes to thicken, then stir in a quarter of the parmesan. Pour one-third of the sauce into a 20cm x 30cm oven dish, followed by half the roasted veg, a quarter of the parmesan and half the pasta. Repeat, ending with sauce and the remaining parmesan. Scatter over torn mozzarella. Bake in the oven for 40 minutes until golden on top and crisp around the edges.

MUSHROOM, MASCARPONE & SAGE RISOTTO

Serves 4-6

- 20g dried porcini mushrooms
- 1 carrot, finely chopped
- 1 celery stalk, finely chopped
- 1 onion, finely chopped
- 2 garlic cloves, finely chopped
- 10 sage leaves, chopped
- 2 tbsp olive oil
- 300g risotto rice
- 200ml dry vermouth
- 650-850ml veg stock
- 250g mixed wild mushrooms, roughly chopped
- 15g butter
- 150g mascarpone
- Grated parmesan, to serve

1 Soak the dried porcini mushrooms in 100ml boiling water. Meanwhile, place the carrot, celery, onion, garlic, half the sage, olive oil and a pinch of salt in a large, deep pan over a low heat and cook until soft. Add the rice and cook for another 2 minutes until the rice is translucent. Add the vermouth and allow to reduce before stirring in the stock, ladle by ladle, allowing it to be absorbed before adding more.
2 Add the porcini and the liquid they were soaking in. Gently fry the wild mushrooms in a separate pan with the butter for 5 minutes, or until soft. When the risotto is al dente, stir in the mascarpone, the wild mushrooms and the remaining sage. Season and serve sprinkled with grated parmesan.

SHETLAND SALMON & FENNEL SALAD

SHETLAND SALMON & FENNEL SALAD

Recipe by Fifteen London
Serves 4

- 4 x 200g salmon steaks - cut across the bone (called darnes - ask your fishmonger to do this)
- 75ml olive oil
- 1 head of fennel, leafy fronds picked and reserved
- 2-3 lemons
- ½ bunch of mint, leaves picked and finely sliced
- 100g wild rocket (optional)

1 Heat your barbecue or griddle pan to a medium heat. Brush the salmon with a little olive oil, and season. Place on the barbecue or griddle and cook for 4 minutes each side. Test with a skewer. (Touch the skewer to your upper lip: if it's warm to hot the salmon is cooked.)
2 Meanwhile, slice the fennel as finely as you can (use a mandolin if you have one) and place in a bowl. Very finely slice

1 lemon (this one's optional) and add to the bowl with the fennel and the rest of the olive oil. Zest the second lemon and add to the bowl, cut the lemon in half and squeeze in the juice of one half. Add the mint, the rocket, if using, and season.
3 Once the salmon is cooked, squeeze over the juice of the last lemon. Serve with the crunchy lemon and fennel salad, and scatter over the fennel tops.

....

KERALAN SEAFOOD CURRY

"This a classic Keralan seafood curry, and for anyone that's never had a fish curry before, please try it - it's absolutely delicious," says Jamie. "If you really must, you can swap the fish for chicken. It'll still be lovely, but you're rather missing the point!"
Serves 4-6

- Vegetable oil
- 2 tsp mustard seeds
- 1 tsp fenugreek seeds
- 1 green chilli, deseeded, finely sliced
- 1 handful of fresh or dried curry leaves, crumbled
- 2 thumb-sized pieces of fresh ginger, peeled and coarsely grated
- 3 onions, peeled and finely chopped
- 12 large prawns
- 1 tsp chilli powder
- 1 tsp turmeric
- 1 handful of ripe yellow cherry tomatoes, chopped
- 1 x 400ml tin light coconut milk
- 400g monkfish fillets, skinned and pin-boned
- 1 heaped tbsp tamarind paste
- 75g baby spinach, optional
- A few sprigs of fresh coriander, leaves picked and chopped
- 2 limes, to serve

1 Heat a good glug of oil in a pan and add the mustard seeds. Once they start to pop, add the fenugreek, green chilli, curry leaves and ginger. Stir fry for a few minutes until it smells fantastic, then add the onions.
2 Cook for another 10 minutes, or until the onion is soft and turning golden, then add the prawns. Cook for a couple of minutes on each side then add the chilli powder, turmeric and tomatoes. Cook for a couple of minutes, then add 1-2 wine glasses (200ml) of water and the coconut milk. Simmer for about 5 minutes until thickened slightly, then season carefully with sea salt.
3 Add the monkfish and tamarind and simmer for 6-10 minutes. Stir through the spinach just before serving, sprinkle with the chopped coriander leaves and serve with lime wedges.

CLASSIC KERALAN CURRY

KERALAN SEAFOOD CURRY

The rice for all occasions

Whether you want pure Basmati, healthy wholegrain, rice that is steamed to perfection in two minutes or a selection of tasty and nutritious options for the kids – Tilda is the ultimate store-cupboard essential

Tilda Basmati rice is, for those in the know, one of their best-kept secrets!

Combining its superfood status with incredible versatility, Tilda Basmati rice is perfect for everything, from quick family meals to dinner party connoisseurship. Savoury or sweet, hot or cold, Basmati rice is delicious, nutritious and goes with almost any dish.

To ensure your Basmati rice is always light and fluffy, Tilda select the purest grains, removing broken and discoloured grains to guarantee only the finest rice is in each Tilda pack. Broken grains release starch while cooking causing the rice to become sticky and clump. As well as selecting the best quality rice, a top tip is to rinse your rice before cooking to be assured of the perfect results. Not many people know Basmati improves with age, Tilda take time to store the Basmati as this enhances the beautiful Basmati aroma. Another reason why Basmati rice is the ultimate cupboard essential. For those wanting to be a little more healthy, the delicately nutty Wholegrain Basmati is a great menu addition providing extra nutrition and a source of fibre.

For when there is less time for cooking, but you still want something deliciously creative there is a range of 2-minute Tilda Steamed Basmati recipe rice. The award winning range of 18 varieties includes Pilau, Sweet Chilli & Lime, Coconut, Mushroom and Lime & Coriander, so you are bound to find favourites for all the family. Every recipe combines the finest Tilda Basmati and the best natural ingredients in really tasty ways. For those that enjoy the extra healthiness and taste of Wholegrain Basmati, there are recipes such as Roasted Pepper & Courgette and Butternut Squash, which are also perfect for making risottos healthier.

For your little ones, and maybe even fussy eaters, the Tilda Kids 'rice & veggies' range is gentle on their tums and taste buds. Each Tilda Kids pouch also provides '1-of-your-5-a-day'; the child-friendly range includes Cheese & Tomato, Mild & Sweet Curry, Sunshine Vegetable and Sweet Vegetable & Wholegrain. They are the perfect accompaniment to all their favourite meals and only take 40 seconds in the microwave, so great for busy feeding times!

Visit tilda.com for delicious recipe ideas for the whole family.

JAMIE'S BETTER BURGER

this order: onion, yoghurt sauce, burger, salsa, a few pickled chillies, and a slice or two of lettuce. Top with the bun lid.

SHEPHERD'S BIRYANI

Serves 8

- Olive oil
- 2 onions, finely sliced
- 2 celery stalks, finely chopped
- 3 carrots, finely chopped
- 2 garlic cloves, finely sliced
- ½ x 283g jar of rogan josh paste
- 1 tbsp tomato purée
- 500g leftover roast lamb, shredded
- 1 litre hot chicken stock
- 1 large bunch of coriander, leaves picked and chopped
- Zest and juice of 1 lemon
- 400g basmati rice
- 2 tbsp olive oil
- 2 tsp brown mustard seeds
- A handful of fresh curry leaves
- 4 cloves

1 Place a large pan over a medium heat. Add a little oil, the vegetables, garlic and a splash of water. Cook for 10-15 minutes, stirring occasionally, until soft.
2 Stir in the curry paste, tomato purée and the shredded meat. Cook for 1-2 minutes, then pour in the hot stock. (If you have any lamb bones, add one now for extra flavour.) Bring the sauce to the boil, then leave to simmer with the lid ajar for 1 hour. Remove the lid and cook for another 15-30 minutes, until it has reduced. Turn off the heat (remove any bones) and season. Stir in the coriander and a squeeze of lemon juice.
3 Cook the rice in a generous amount of salted water for about 10 minutes. Drain, rinse and refresh under cold water until cool. Preheat the oven to 200C/gas 6.
4 Meanwhile, in a small pan heat a dash of oil with the mustard seeds, crumbled curry leaves, cloves and lemon zest until fragrant. Toss with half the cooled rice.
5 Spoon the meat sauce into the bottom of an ovenproof dish, then top with the plain rice. Finish with a layer of the flavoured rice. Bake for 25 minutes, or until crunchy on the top and hot through.

JAMIE'S BETTER BURGER

This burger has a mixture of lean minced beef, and a yoghurt sauce (instead of mayo), so it tastes fresh and zippy, but the fat content is lower.
Serves 4

- 200g good-quality minced beef
- 200g lean minced beef
- 2 tsp olive oil, plus a little extra
- 3 large onions, thinly sliced
- 4 burger buns, split
- Yellow pickled chillies and little gem lettuce, to serve

Special yoghurt sauce

- 60g 0% fat plain yoghurt
- ½ tsp English mustard
- A squeeze of lemon juice

Salsa rossa

- 2 ripe tomatoes, skinned, deseeded
- 1 jarred red pepper
- ½ red chilli, deseeded
- Sherry vinegar
- Extra-virgin olive oil
- 2 parsley sprigs, leaves chopped

1 Put the beef in a bowl with about ½ teaspoon of salt and 1 teaspoon of pepper. With clean hands, scrunch and mix well. Divide into 4 and shape into burgers about 2cm thick. Drizzle with a tiny bit of extra oil. Chill, covered, until needed, to help them to firm up.
2 Meanwhile, heat 2 teaspoons of oil in a pan on a medium-low heat. Add the onion and cook for 20-30 minutes till dark and sticky. Add a little water if it looks too dry.
3 For the sauce, combine all the ingredients and adjust to taste.
4 For the salsa rossa, put the tomato, pepper and chilli on a board, then chop and mix it all together. Add a splash of vinegar and oil, and the parsley. Chop and mix into a chunky salsa.
5 Preheat a large griddle or frying pan for about 4 minutes over a high heat, then reduce to medium. Add the burgers and press lightly with a spatula. Cook for 5-6 minutes each side, in batches if needed.
6 Toast the buns on the cut side only. Assemble the ingredients on the bun in

ONE-PAN BREAKFAST

MEDITERRANEAN BRAISED BEEF

A TASTE OF THE MED

To bring a touch of Mediterranean sunshine to any season, keep some nice olives, a jar of tomato passata and some herbs handy for a quick sauce full of summer flavours

ONE-PAN BREAKFAST

Serves 2

- Olive oil
- 1 pork sausage
- A 2cm-thick slice of black pudding
- 2 rashers of smoked streaky bacon
- A handful of mushrooms, roughly chopped
- 4 cherry tomatoes
- 2 large eggs
- Toast and condiments, to serve

1 Preheat the grill to high. Add a little oil to a 24cm pan over a high heat. Split the sausage down the middle and add to the pan with the black pudding and bacon. Leave it for a couple of minutes to crisp up then flip over. If anything looks done, just take it out of the pan.
2 Add the mushrooms and tomatoes, pour away any excess fat, then return any meat you removed to the pan. Spread everything out, make 2 gaps and crack in the eggs; tilt the pan so the whites surround everything. Cook for 1 minute, then place under the grill for 2 minutes, or until the eggs are done to your liking.
3 Serve in the pan with hot toast and your favourite condiments.

MEDITERRANEAN BRAISED BEEF

This recipes uses topside steaks instead of more expensive cuts, and they taste just as great here.
Serves 6

- 6 x 125g topside minute steaks
- 1 tbsp dried oregano
- Grated zest and juice of 1 lemon
- 4 tinned or jarred anchovies in oil
- 150g stale bread
- 40g feta cheese
- Olive oil
- 2 garlic cloves, sliced
- 12 olives, stones removed
- 800g tinned plum tomatoes
- 1 bunch of basil, leaves chopped, stalks finely chopped

1 Preheat the oven to 170C/gas 3. Sprinkle the steaks with the oregano and a pinch of salt and pepper, then finely grate over the lemon zest.
2 Whiz up the anchovies, bread, feta and a drizzle of anchovy oil in a food processor till you have fine crumbs. Scatter the mixture over 1 side of the steaks, reserving a handful for later, then roll the steaks up around the filling and secure with cocktail sticks.
3 Add a glug of olive oil to a casserole pan that will fit the steaks snugly, add the steaks and cook over a medium heat. Once golden-brown underneath, turn them and add the garlic, olives, tomatoes, basil stalks and a little salt and pepper. Break up the tomatoes with a spoon, add 250ml water, then put the lid on.
4 Transfer to the oven and cook for 1½ hours, or till the meat is tender. Remove the lid, scatter over the remaining bread mixture and drizzle with a little oil. Turn the oven up to 180C/gas 4 and cook for a further 20–30 minutes, till golden brown on top and bubbling up from underneath.
5 Divide the meat between plates, squeeze the lemon juice into the sauce and add the chopped basil leaves. Taste for seasoning and adjust as needed, then spoon the sauce over the meat.

BUTTERNUT SQUASH
A great source of vitamins A and C, the squash is a relative of the courgette and cucumber. Its vibrant orange flesh sits as happily with roast meats as it does in pasta parcels or accompanied by tangy goat's cheese

CHICKEN & HERB BISCUITS

CHICKEN & HERB BISCUITS

Recipe by Maria Helm Sinskey
Serves 6-8

- 15ml olive oil
- 2 celery stalks, trimmed and finely chopped
- 1 onion, finely chopped
- 3 carrots, cut into 2.5cm pieces
- 300g peeled butternut squash, cut into 2.5cm chunks
- 1 bay leaf
- 1 litre chicken stock
- 700g cooked chicken, (a mix of light and dark meat), diced or shredded
- 2 tbsp flour

Herb biscuits

- 230g plain flour
- 1 tbsp baking powder
- 1½ tsp sea salt
- 1 tsp finely chopped thyme leaves
- ½ tsp finely chopped rosemary
- 110g unsalted butter, chilled, cut into chunks
- 240ml single cream

1 For the biscuits, combine the dry ingredients and herbs. Work in the butter with your fingers until the mixture forms big crumbs, the size of small peas.
2 Add the cream and mix until evenly incorporated. The dough should be slightly sticky. Turn out onto a lightly floured board and pat into a 2.5cm-thick circle. Using a 5cm-diameter cutter, cut into 12-14 rounds. Set aside to cook with the chicken.
3 Heat the olive oil in a large saucepan over a medium heat, and add the celery and onion. Cook, stirring, about 4-5 minutes, until the vegetables start to turn golden.
4 Add the carrots and squash and sauté until they begin to soften. Add the bay leaf and chicken stock. Bring the whole broth to a boil then reduce to a simmer for 20 minutes, or until the vegetables are tender.
5 Preheat the oven to 190C/gas 5. In a bowl, whisk 120ml cold water and 2 tablespoons of flour until combined. Add a cup of the hot broth to the flour and water and whisk well. Strain the mixture and whisk it back into the broth.
6 Bring the broth to a boil. Add the chicken, and season. Reduce the heat and simmer for 5 minutes.
7 Pour the broth into a 2.8-litre baking dish. Top the chicken with the uncooked biscuits and bake for 35-40 minutes until the biscuits are golden and cooked through, and the broth is bubbling.

CARDAMOM-BAKED PORK TENDERLOIN

Serves 4

- Seeds from 6 cardamom pods
- 2 garlic cloves
- 1 tbsp olive oil
- About 500g pork tenderloin
- 1 gala apple, cut into wedges
- 2 figs, cut into wedges
- 150ml dry cider

1 Preheat the oven to 160C/gas 2½. Bash the cardamom seeds, garlic and a pinch of salt with a pestle and mortar. Stir in the olive oil and rub the paste all over the tenderloin. Place the meat in a roasting pan. Arrange the apple and figs in the pan, too, then pour in the cider and roast in the oven for 25-35 minutes, until the meat is cooked through. Slice the meat and spoon over the cooking liquid before serving with the fruit.

CARDAMOM-BAKED PORK TENDERLOIN

USE FORAGED FRUITS

BRAMBLE TRIFLE

BLACKBERRIES Nothing marks the dawn of autumn better than purpled hands and a foraged hoard. Eat immediately or cook in an apple crumble for a classic pairing. Blackberries and other berries make excellent jams and jellies to see you through the winter

BRAMBLE JELLY WITH JERSEY CREAM

BRAMBLE TRIFLE

Serves 10
- 200g ready-made madeira sponge
- 100ml sweet sherry
- 100g amaretti biscuits
- 300g brambles
- 300ml double cream

Custard
- 500ml milk
- 150ml double cream
- 8 egg yolks
- 75g sugar
- 1 heaped tbsp cornflour

1 For the custard, add the milk and cream to a pan and place over a medium heat. Meanwhile, whisk the egg yolks, sugar and cornflour together until smooth. As soon as the milk mixture starts to bubble at the edges, pour it into the egg yolk mix, whisking as you go. Return the mix to the pan and place back over the heat. Stir the custard with a spatula until it thickens, then take off the heat and pour into a clean bowl. Cover with greaseproof paper and set aside to cool completely.
2 Break the sponge into chunks and layer over the base of a glass trifle dish. Splash on the sherry and let the cake soak it up. Crumble over three-quarters of the amaretti, then cover with the brambles, saving the best-looking ones (about a third) to scatter over the top. Spoon over the cooled custard over the top and

smooth it out to create an even surface.
3 Whip the double cream to soft peaks, then spoon it over the custard and smooth out. Decorate the trifle with the rest of the brambles, then put it in the fridge for 3 hours to set.
4 Just before serving, crumble over the rest of the amaretti. To serve, scoop big spoonfuls into bowls, making sure you reach the bottom, to get all of the layers.

BRAMBLE JELLY WITH JERSEY CREAM

Serves 6
- 400g sugar
- 6 bay leaves
- 2kg brambles, fresh or frozen and defrosted
- 1-2 gelatine leaves
- Jersey cream
- Ground cinnamon

1 In a large saucepan, bring the sugar, bay leaves and 600ml water to the boil.

Add brambles and cook, covered, over a low heat for 8-10 minutes, or until the brambles have burst.
2 Cool a little, then strain through a sieve into a bowl, pressing with a ladle to extract as much juice as possible. Strain again through a fine conical sieve, or rinse the sieve you've just used, line with clean, wet muslin, and use that. Measure the juice – the amount will depend on the size and ripeness of the berries.
3 Use 1 gelatine leaf for every 150ml juice. This will give you a soft-set jelly; for a firmer result, use 1 extra leaf. Soften the leaves in a bowl of cold water for 5 minutes, then remove and squeeze out the water. Put the leaves in a pan with a quarter of the juice and warm over a medium heat until the gelatine melts. Add the rest of the juice off the heat.
4 Pour the jelly mixture into a jug then divide evenly between 6 glass serving dishes and chill in the fridge until set. Serve with Jersey cream and a pinch of ground cinnamon on top.

CHESTNUT CRÊPES WITH BRAMBLES

CHESTNUT CRÊPES WITH BRAMBLES

Serves 10

- 45g butter, plus extra for frying
- 525ml milk
- 1 tbsp sugar
- 75g flour
- 150g chestnut flour
- 3 eggs, beaten
- A few knobs of butter
- Vanilla ice cream, to serve

Sautéed brambles

- 1½ tbsp caster sugar
- 1 small cinnamon stick
- A splash of whisky
- 525g blackberries

1 Place the butter and milk in a small saucepan with the sugar and a good pinch of salt. Warm gently until the butter has melted and the sugar dissolved, then turn off the heat.
2 Tip the plain flour and chestnut flour into a mixing bowl, make a well in the centre and add the eggs. Gradually whisk the flour into the eggs, until the mixture is quite stiff. Add a splash of the warm milk to loosen, then keep whisking it in until you have a smooth batter the texture of single cream.
3 For the sautéed brambles, heat a stainless-steel pan over a medium heat, add the sugar, and just enough water to dissolve it, and the cinnamon. Cook the syrup till light brown (not a full caramel colour) then add a splash of whisky, and take off the heat.
4 Stir the berries into the hot syrup, then leave to cool. You should end up with soft, sticky fruit in a delicious dark red juice – if there isn't enough juice, add a bit more water to the pan.
5 Heat a 25cm nonstick frying pan over a medium heat. When hot, add a knob of butter and swirl it around the pan until melted and sizzling. Add a ladle of batter, quickly swirl it to coat and form a thin layer on the surface of the pan. Cook for about a minute, or until the surface is set with little holes in it, then flip with a palette knife, cook for another 30 seconds and tip onto a plate.
6 Wipe the pan with kitchen paper, add a small knob of butter and repeat. Keep the finished crêpes warm in a low oven.
7 To serve, place a crêpe on a warm plate, spread with a few spoonfuls of bramble sauce, fold into quarters, drizzle with bramble juice, add a scoop of ice cream and dust lightly with icing sugar.

MACADAMIA & HONEY TART
Recipe by Stephanie Alexander
Serves 10-12

- 60g butter
- 100g flour
- 60g caster sugar
- 1 tsp grated orange zest
- 3 tbsp strained orange juice

Macadamia & honey filling

- 150g-200g unsalted macadamia nuts
- 2 eggs
- 40g caster sugar
- 60ml light corn syrup or golden syrup
- 60ml single-flower honey
- 20g butter, melted
- ½ tsp grated orange zest

1 Preheat the oven to 200C/gas 6. Pulse the first five ingredients in a processor until the pastry forms a ball. Wrap in clingfilm and flatten into a round. Chill for at least 1 hour, then roll out between 2 sheets of clingfilm. Remove the top sheet of clingfilm and invert the pastry into a shallow, 22cm round loose-bottomed tart tin. Peel off the other sheet of clingfilm and gently press the pastry into the tin. Let the excess hang over the side of the tin, untrimmed. Line with baking paper, fill with baking weights and blind bake for 10 minutes, until the sides turn golden. Remove the paper and weights and bake the pastry for 5 more minutes to set the base, but watch it closely as the zest can make it scorch. Cool, then trim the excess pastry.
2 Preheat the oven to 180C/gas 4. For the filling, scatter the nuts over the pastry case to form quite a solid base. Whisk together the remaining ingredients and pour over the nuts.
3 Bake the tart on the lowest oven rack for 30 minutes, until golden and puffed up, then move to the top shelf and cook for 15 minutes, till the filling is brown and bubbling. Leave to cool before cutting.

MACADAMIA & HONEY TART

GLUTEN-FREE APPLE &
ALMOND CUPCAKES

PEAR CLAFOUTIS

PEARS & PECORINO

Part pudding, part cheese course, this simple recipe makes a pleasing end to any meal – or a snack or starter.
Adjust the quantities to taste.

- A few ripe pears, peeled and cored
- Sugar, to taste
- A few slices of pecorino cheese
- 1-2 bay leaves (optional)
- Walnut bread, to serve (optional)

1 Cut the pears into quarters or halves, depending on size. Heat a griddle pan over a high heat until searing, and place the pears on the griddle, cooking both sides until soft and charred.
2 Arrange the pears in an ovenproof gratin dish. Sprinkle with sugar, top with pecorino slices and a couple of bay leaves, if you like. Place under a hot grill until the cheese melts. Serve with slices of fresh or toasted walnut bread.

GLUTEN-FREE PEAR & ALMOND CUPCAKES

Serves 20-24

- 200g gluten-free flour
- 100g ground almonds
- A pinch of salt
- 2 tsp baking powder
- ½ tsp ground cardamom
- 5 eggs
- 2 tbsp vegetable oil
- 200g sugar
- 2 crisp pears, cored and chopped

1 Preheat the oven to 180C/gas 4 and line two 12-hole muffin trays with cupcake cases. Combine the dry ingredients in a bowl. Beat the eggs, oil and sugar together till light and fluffy. Beat in the dry ingredients then stir in the pear. Spoon the batter into the cases and bake for 20-30 minutes until firm, and the tops are light golden.

PEAR CLAFOUTIS

Clafoutis is such an easy pudding to make, and you can substitute any fruit you like, or that's in season. Just make sure not to overcook it – you want the centre to be pale, not too tough.
Serves 4

- 4 small blush pears, quartered
- 50g sugar
- 2 star anise
- 1 cinnamon stick
- 3 eggs
- 100g sugar
- 2-3 drops vanilla extract
- 50g flour
- 50ml double cream
- 100ml milk

1 Put the pears in a pan with the sugar, anise, cinnamon and 500ml water. Bring to the boil, then simmer for 10-20 minutes, until the pears are tender. Let them cool in the liquid.
2 Preheat oven to 180C/gas 4. In a bowl, beat eggs, sugar and vanilla till fluffy, fold in flour and a pinch of salt then beat in the double cream and milk. Place the pears into baking dishes, pour over batter and bake for 15 minutes, until the edges are golden and the centre has just begun to set – you don't want it be runny, or hard like a cake.

PEARS Mentioned in the 1086 Doomsday Book as boundary markers, pear trees have been around a while. The fragrant fruit can stand up to a tangy cheese just as well as juicy grapes and apples or earthy walnuts

BAKED FIGS

BANBURY CAKES

FIGS A sweet treat best enjoyed at the end of summer and early autumn. Couple with salty parma ham, creamy goat's cheese or drizzle with honey and nuts

BAKED FIGS
Serves 4

- 1 vanilla pod, split, seeds scraped
- 1 tbsp sugar
- A pinch of ground cinnamon
- 6 figs, halved
- Juice of 1 orange
- 1 tbsp honey
- 20g pistachios, chopped
- 3 mint sprigs, leaves picked
- Ice cream or crème fraîche, to serve

1 Preheat the oven to 180C/gas 4. Grind the vanilla seeds with the sugar and cinnamon in a pestle and mortar.
2 Place the figs in a baking dish and drizzle with the orange juice and honey. Add the pistachios, tuck in the mint and sprinkle with vanilla sugar. Bake for 15 minutes, until tender. Serve warm, with ice cream, yoghurt or crème fraîche.

BANBURY CAKES
Serves 10

- 50g butter, softened
- 1 tbsp runny honey
- 12 gratings of whole nutmeg
- ½ tsp ground allspice
- ½ tsp ground cinnamon
- 50g each of raisins, currants and candied citrus peel
- 1 tbsp dark rum
- Flour, for dusting
- 300g puff pastry
- 1 egg, beaten
- 3 tbsp granulated sugar

1 Preheat the oven to 180C/gas 4. Line a baking tray with baking paper. In a large bowl, cream the butter and honey, then stir in the spices. Add the dried fruit, candied peel, rum and stir to combine.
2 Lightly flour a work surface and roll out the pastry to about 2.5mm thick. Using a 10cm pastry cutter cut out 10 circles. If you have to roll it out and cut it again, be sure to fold it over itself rather than scrunch it as you will damage the layers.
3 Spoon the filling into the centre of each disc, leaving a little space around the edges. Brush either side of the filling with a little egg. Bring the sides of the pastry up into the middle and crimp slightly to make little purses.
4 Turn the cakes over so the fold is on the bottom and very gently roll them into oval shapes with your rolling pin, being careful not to burst them.
5 Place the cakes on the tray and, with the tip of a knife, make 3 little cuts on each. Brush with the beaten egg and sprinkle with granulated sugar.
6 Cook for 25–30 minutes until golden and firm. Transfer to a wire rack to cool slightly before serving warm.

GINGERBREAD & BUTTER PUDDING
Serves 6

- 25g butter
- 500g stale gingerbread, in 1cm slices
- 75g raisins
- Finely grated zest of ½ orange
- 400ml whole milk
- 2 eggs
- 50g soft light brown sugar
- A pinch of cinnamon

1 Preheat the oven to 180C/gas 4. Butter one side of each gingerbread slice and layer them, butter-side down, in a 25cm round baking dish, alternating with layers of raisins and zest.
2 Beat the milk, eggs, sugar and cinnamon together in a bowl, and then pour over the gingerbread. Leave for 15 minutes to soak. Top with a little extra milk if too dry. Bake for 30–45 minutes until golden and set, and serve warm.

USE UP LEFTOVERS

COCONUT RICE PUDDING WITH ROASTED FRUIT

GARIBALDIS

APPLE, CINNAMON & OAT CAKE

COCONUT RICE PUDDING WITH ROASTED FRUIT

Serves 10-12

- 200g pudding rice
- 400ml tin light coconut milk
- 800ml semi-skimmed milk
- 2 tbsp golden caster sugar
- 1 vanilla pod, split lengthways

Flavoured sugar

- ½ a cinnamon stick
- 3 cardamom pods
- 3 cloves
- 1cm piece of fresh ginger, peeled and finely grated
- 80g light brown muscovado sugar

Roasted fruit

- 1 mango, peeled, stoned and cut into 1cm wedges
- 1 pineapple, peeled, cored and cut into 1–2cm wedges
- Zest and juice of 1 orange

1 Preheat the oven to 200C/gas 6. Place a pan over a medium heat and add the rice, both milks, sugar and vanilla pod. Simmer for 25–30 minutes, until creamy and tender, stirring occasionally.
2 Meanwhile, in a pestle and mortar, bash the cinnamon, cardamom and cloves together until fine, then grind in the ginger and brown sugar.
3 In a large roasting dish toss the mango and pineapple with the flavoured sugar,

orange zest and juice and bake for 15–20 minutes, until lightly caramelised. Serve the rice pudding in bowls and spoon over the fruit and juices.

GARIBALDIS

Makes 20 biscuits

- 100g butter, melted
- 100g icing sugar
- 100g flour
- 100g (about 3 medium) egg whites
- 200g currants

1 Beat together the butter, icing sugar and flour with electric beaters until smooth. Slowly beat through the egg whites with a wooden spoon, then fold in the currants. Don't worry if the dough is quite wet. Transfer the mixture to a small bowl and put in the fridge to chill for 1 hour.
2 Line a baking sheet with some greaseproof paper. Place the biscuit mixture on the prepared sheet and spread out into a rectangle. Top with another sheet of greaseproof paper and place another baking sheet on top. Using something heavy, such as a brick wrapped in foil, press down on the baking sheet to flatten the mixture. Chill for another 30 minutes.
3 Meanwhile, preheat the oven to 180C/ gas 4. Remove the biscuits from the

fridge and bake, with the weighted-down tray still on top, for 25–30 minutes or until golden brown. Cut into rectangular slices while soft.

APPLE, CINNAMON & OAT CAKE

Serves 8-10

- 180g butter
- 140g demerara sugar
- 3 eggs
- 180g self-raising flour
- 2 tsp baking powder
- 2 tsp ground cinnamon
- 2 apples
- 2 tbsp oats
- Icing sugar for dusting

1 Preheat the oven to 170C/gas 3. Beat together the butter and sugar until light and fluffy. Gradually beat in the eggs, then the dry ingredients. Peel and grate 1 apple and fold into the cake mix. Pour half the mix into a greased, lined 18cm cake tin. Finely slice the other apple, place half the slices in the tin, cover with the rest of the cake mix and top with the remaining slices. Scatter the oats over the top. Bake for 45 minutes, then cover the cake with tin foil and pop back in the oven to bake for 30 more minutes, until a skewer comes out clean. Allow to cool, then dust with icing sugar.

GINGER MARTINI

BRAMBLE GIN

DECADENT HOT CHOCOLATE

This is rich, boozy, prefect for cold nights and definitely for adults only!

Serves 2

- 285ml (½ pint) milk
- ¾ tbsp icing sugar
- 1 tbsp organic cocoa powder
- 25g 70%-cocoa chocolate, finely grated
- A pinch of ground cinnamon
- A pinch of fine sea salt
- 2 shots of rum or whisky
- 15ml double cream, to serve (optional)

1 Place the milk in a large saucepan over a medium heat, and gently bring almost to the boil.
2 Meanwhile, put all the remaining ingredients except the alcohol and cream in a large jar and shake well.
3 Whisk the chocolate mixture into the pan of hot milk, and leave to bubble away for a few minutes. Add your booze and let it simmer for a few more minutes, then pour into cups. If you're feeling decadent, swirl through some cream, and serve.

GINGER MARTINI

Serves 2

- Ice
- 100ml vodka
- 40ml ginger syrup (see below)
- Zest and juice of 1 lime
- 1cm piece of ginger, finely grated

Ginger syrup

- 4cm ginger, peeled and sliced
- 25g sugar

1 Make the ginger syrup: put the ginger, sugar and 50ml water in a small pan. Bring to the boil, then simmer for about 5 minutes. Leave to cool, then strain through a sieve.
2 Half fill a cocktail shaker with ice, add the vodka, ginger syrup and lime juice. Squeeze the juice from the grated ginger into the shaker. Put on the lid and shake. Strain through a fine sieve into 2 chilled martini glasses. Garnish with lime zest.

BRAMBLE GIN

A brilliant thing to have in the cupboard, for fireside sipping. It also makes an excellent Christmas gift, so get picking. You can use whisky instead of gin, if you prefer.

Makes 1.6 litres

- 500g brambles
- 250g sugar
- 3 bay leaves
- 3 cloves
- 1 litre gin

1 Put the brambles in a food processor and blitz until puréed.
2 Smash the sugar, bay leaves and cloves together with a pestle and mortar until combined.
3 Spoon the puréed brambles and sugar mixture into a 1.5-litre jar and pour the gin on top. Seal the jar so it's airtight, and shake well. Leave in a dark cupboard for at least 1 month for the flavours to combine. Shake now and then, whenever you think of it.
4 Strain the gin through a clean piece of wet muslin into a jug, then pour into clean, sterilised bottles and seal tightly. The bramble gin will keep in a cool, dark place for several months (if not longer!). Shake before serving on its own, or stir into champagne or cocktails.

Welsh Lamb.
Prepared over centuries.
Cooked in minutes.

Welsh Lamb has taken hundreds of years to prepare. Our craggy slopes, glacial hillsides and unique climate produce deliciously sweet grass, which produces deliciously sweet Welsh Lamb — it's just one of the reasons why we've been awarded PGI status. But whilst Welsh Lamb may have taken thousands of years to prepare, it takes far less time to cook. Juicy Welsh Lamb chops, delicious meatballs or sizzling stir-fry can all be prepared in just 20 minutes or less, but how long you take to enjoy them is entirely up to you.

WINTER
in association with
Welsh Lamb

To find out more about PGI, or for more news, recipes and information

WELSH

WINTER

is for warming soups,
slow-cooked meats, root
vegetables and deep spicy
flavours followed by
comforting puds

CURRY TOMATO SOUP

CURRY TOMATO SOUP
Recipe by Barbara Kafka
Serves 2

- 30g butter
- 1 small onion, finely chopped
- 3 tbsp curry powder
- 1 tbsp sweet paprika
- 625g tinned Italian plum tomatoes, puréed with their juice, or passata
- 500ml beef, chicken or veg stock
- 1 tbsp lemon juice

1 Melt the butter in a large saucepan over a low heat. Stir in the onion and sweat until soft and translucent, but not coloured. Add the curry powder and paprika and continue to cook, stirring constantly, for 3 minutes.
2 Stir in the tomatoes and the stock. Bring to the boil, then simmer for 5 minutes. Taste the soup and season generously. It can be chilled and kept for a day or so at this point. To serve cold, stir in the lemon juice or reheat the mixture before adding the juice.

RICH CHICKEN SOUP WITH MATZO BALLS
Recipe by Paul Levy
Chicken soup is an age-old comfort dish but studies suggest it may actually offer medicinal benefits for colds – just what you want in winter.
Serves 4-8

- 1kg chicken backs, wings and carcasses, roasted
- 4 garlic cloves, smashed
- A few white onions, halved, skins on
- A handful of leek tops
- 1 carrot, scrubbed
- 1 celery heart
- A handful of parsley stalks
- A glug of white wine (optional)
- A pinch of crushed black peppercorns

Matzo balls

- 120g matzo meal
- 30g ground almonds
- A pinch of ground ginger
- 2 heaped tbsp rendered goose, duck or chicken fat, softened
- 2 eggs, separated, plus 6 egg whites
- 5 tbsp chicken soup
- Chopped chives or parsley, to serve

1 Place all the soup ingredients in a large pan with enough cold water to cover. Bring to the boil then reduce to a simmer. Skim off any impurities – do this a few times until the stock is clear and golden. Strain, discard any solids, and season.
2 Leave the soup in the fridge until needed – any fat will solidify on the surface for easy removal. If making this ahead you can freeze this once cooled.
3 To make the matzo balls, combine all the dry ingredients in a bowl, then fork in your chosen fat. Beat the egg yolks into the mixture, one at a time, and then 5 tablespoons of the chicken soup.
4 Beat the 8 egg whites until they hold a peak, then stir half the egg whites into the matzo mixture. Fold in the rest with a metal spoon. Chill in the fridge for at least 3 hours, or overnight.
5 With wet hands, form the mixture into 8 balls, then drop into lots of simmering salted water for at least 30 minutes. The balls will double in size, and keep in their water for a day or so. To reheat, bring the water slowly back to a simmer.
6 To serve, place 1 or 2 matzo balls into a bowl, ladle the soup over and sprinkle with some chopped chives or parsley.

RICH CHICKEN SOUP WITH MATZO BALLS

TURKEY CHOWDER

CHORIZO & SPLIT PEA SOUP

TURKEY CHOWDER

This super tasty dish is a great way to use up leftover roast turkey and veg.

Serves 4-6

- Olive oil
- 4 smoked streaky bacon rashers, finely chopped, plus extra to serve
- 3 onions, finely sliced
- 3 garlic cloves, finely chopped
- A bunch of flat-leaf parsley, leaves chopped, stalks finely chopped
- 1 cooked jacket potato or 200g leftover roast veg, chopped
- 500g leftover roast turkey, shredded
- 1 red pepper, deseeded and chopped
- 2 heaped tsp cayenne pepper
- 1 tsp sweet smoked paprika
- 1 litre chicken stock
- 3 large handfuls of frozen sweetcorn
- 20-50ml single cream, to taste
- 40g grated cheddar cheese
- Crackers or thin toast, to serve
- Chilli sauce, to serve (optional)

1 Heat a drizzle of olive oil in a large pan over a medium heat. Add the bacon, onion, garlic and parsley stalks and fry for 5-10 minutes, until sticky. Invest a bit of time - you want it to be really dark to get the best flavour in your chowder. (Reserve some bacon pieces to garnish.)
2 Add the potato or roast veg, any dark turkey meat and the red pepper. Add the cayenne pepper and smoked paprika

and fry for about 10 minutes.
3 Add the stock, then bring to the boil. Blitz briefly with a hand blender, to thicken. Add the corn, any white turkey meat, and dash of cream. Let it simmer for a few minutes, then season. Lastly, stir in the parsley leaves and cheese.
4 Serve with thin slices of toast or smashed crackers, extra bacon pieces, and a splash of chilli sauce, if you like.

CHORIZO & SPLIT PEA SOUP

Serves 4-6

- 1 red onion, finely sliced
- 4 garlic cloves, finely chopped
- 2 tbsp olive oil
- 1 red chilli, finely chopped
- 1 red pepper, deseeded and sliced
- 250g chorizo, sliced
- 1-2 tsp smoked paprika
- 1 tbsp thyme leaves
- 400g yellow split peas, soaked in cold water for 2 hours, and drained
- 1.5 litres chicken or veg stock
- Juice of ½ lemon

1 Fry the onion and garlic in the oil for 3 minutes until soft. Add the chilli, pepper and chorizo. After 3 minutes, add the paprika, thyme, peas and stock. Bring to the boil, then simmer for 30 minutes. Stir in the lemon juice and serve with bread.

ASIAN CHICKEN NOODLE BROTH

Serves 6-8

- 1 x 1.6kg chicken
- 400ml tin reduced-fat coconut milk
- 1 tsp turmeric
- 4 nests of egg noodles
- 3cm piece of ginger, peeled and finely sliced (use a mandolin if you have one)
- 2 red chillies, finely sliced
- 2 carrots, finely sliced
- 250g sugar snap peas, finely sliced
- Soy sauce
- Juice of 1 lime
- A small bunch of coriander, chopped

1 Put the chicken in a snug-fitting pot and just cover with boiling water. Add a pinch of salt, cover, and simmer over a medium-low heat for 1½ hours, or until the chicken is falling off the bone.
2 Carefully move the chicken to a board and, when cool enough to handle, pick and shred the meat; discard the bones and skin. Turn the heat up under the broth and reduce to 1.2-1.5 litres.
3 When the broth has reduced, add the chicken, coconut milk, turmeric, and noodles. Cook for 2 minutes, then add the ginger, chillies and veg, and cook for 1 minute, retaining a bit of crunch. Remove from the heat and season with soy sauce and lime juice to taste. Ladle into bowls and top with the coriander.

SPICE IT UP

ASIAN CHICKEN NOODLE BROTH

SMASHED BORLOTTI BEAN BRUSCHETTA

SMASHED BORLOTTI BEAN BRUSCHETTA

Recipe by Jamie's Italian

Serves 4

- 200g dried borlotti beans, soaked overnight in cold water
- 1 celery stalk, chopped into 3
- ½ a small bunch of parsley
- 3 garlic cloves, halved
- 1 lemon, plus the grated zest from ½ lemon
- Olive oil
- A large handful of mint leaves, chopped, plus a few extra sprigs
- 8 slices of ciabatta
- 1 red chilli, deseeded and finely chopped
- 20g marzotica or parmesan, grated

1 Place the beans, celery, parsley, 2 garlic cloves and half the lemon in a large pan and cover with cold water. Bring to the boil, then simmer for 45–60 minutes, until the beans are soft. Remove from the heat, add a pinch of salt to the pan and set aside for 15 minutes. Strain the beans over a bowl to catch the liquid (set aside), and discard the other ingredients.
2 While the beans are warm, squeeze over the other lemon half, season with pepper, drizzle with oil, then stir well. When cool, divide into 2 batches. Stir the chopped mint into one, and blitz the other with a hand blender, loosening with a little cooking liquid and seasoning.
3 To serve, toast the ciabatta and rub with the remaining garlic. Spread with the bean paste and place 2 slices on each plate. Divide the minted beans between the plates and sprinkle over the chilli, mint sprigs, lemon zest and cheese. Drizzle with a little oil and serve warm.

RED ONION TARTS

These are easy, inexpensive and really moreish, ideal for festive entertaining.

Serves 12

- Olive oil
- 500g ready-made butter puff pastry
- Flour, for dusting
- 8 red onions, finely sliced
- 2 garlic cloves, finely sliced
- A few thyme sprigs, leaves picked
- 1 small dried red chilli (optional)
- 50g crumbly goat's cheese

1 Preheat the oven to 190C/gas 5 and grease a baking sheet with a little oil. Roll out the pastry on a floured surface to a 22cm x 30cm rectangle about 5mm thick. Score a 2cm border around the edge, place on the prepared baking sheet and pop in the fridge until needed.
2 For the topping, heat a splash of oil in a pan, add the onions, garlic, half the thyme and crumble in the dried chilli, if using. Cook slowly, covered and stirring occasionally, for about 15 minutes until softened and sweet. Season well.
3 Top the pastry with the onions, spreading them out evenly inside the border. Sprinkle over the remaining thyme and crumble over the goat's cheese. Bake on the bottom of the oven for 20–25 minutes, until the base is crispy. Serve warm in small slices.

RED ONION TARTS

GREAT
FOR
PARTIES

BUBBLE & SQUEAK CROQUETTES

USE UP LEFTOVERS

HAM, BRIE & CRANBERRY PARCELS

BUBBLE & SQUEAK CROQUETTES

Serves 4

- Vegetable oil, for frying
- 3 smoked streaky bacon rashers, chopped
- 2 shallots, finely diced
- 250g sprouts or ½ cabbage, finely chopped
- 400g potatoes, boiled or roasted
- 1 egg yolk
- ¼ nutmeg, grated
- 1 tbsp wholegrain mustard, plus 1 tsp extra to serve
- 2 tbsp flour, plus extra for dusting
- 1 egg, beaten
- A handful of white breadcrumbs
- A few sage sprigs, leaves picked and chopped
- 5 tbsp mayonnaise, to serve

1 In a large frying pan, heat a splash of vegetable oil and cook the bacon over a medium heat for a few minutes. Once it starts to colour, lower the heat and add the shallots. When the bacon is getting crisp, add the sprouts or cabbage and a splash of water, and cover the pan. Allow the sprouts to steam for a few minutes, and then take off the heat.
2 In a bowl, mash the potatoes, then stir in the egg yolk, nutmeg, 1 teaspoon of the mustard, a pinch of black pepper and the bacon mix. With floured hands, mould golf-ball-sized pieces into short cigar shapes. Leave to firm up in the fridge for about 30 minutes.
3 In a bowl, mix the breadcrumbs with the sage. Put the flour in another bowl and the egg in a third. Dust each croquette in flour, then dip in the egg, followed by the sage breadcrumb mix. In a large pan, heat 2cm vegetable oil. Fry the croquettes in batches, until crisp and golden. Mix 1 tablespoon of mustard with the mayonnaise and serve with the hot croquettes.

HAM, BRIE & CRANBERRY PARCELS

Serves 6 as a starter or light lunch

- 30g unsalted butter, melted, plus extra for greasing
- 6 sheets filo pastry, each cut into 3 rectangles
- A small bunch of thyme, leaves picked
- 150g ripe brie, cut into 6
- 75g cooked ham, shredded
- 6 tsp cranberry sauce

1 Preheat the oven to 200C/gas 6 and lightly grease a baking sheet with a little butter. Layer 3 filo rectangles at different angles to make a star shape. Brush each layer of the star with a little melted butter and sprinkle with thyme. Place a piece of brie in the centre, scatter over a little ham and top with a blob of cranberry sauce. Season with salt and pepper to taste. Bring up the sides to make a sack and pinch the top to seal.
2 Brush with butter and sprinkle with thyme. Repeat to make 6 parcels. Bake for about 15 minutes until golden.

Put some quality time on the menu with Welsh Lamb mini rack en croute

We all like to make a big impression - thankfully this show stopper takes very little effort.

Pre-heat your oven to gas mark 6, 200°C, 400°F.

Now pour a splash of olive oil in a large frying pan, add the mini lamb racks and brown on all sides. Once the rack is browned, remove it from pan and allow to cool slightly.

Next, divide pastry into 8 pieces and roll out into a rough square. Carefully place the rack onto the pastry and top with a quarter of the mushrooms and the paté.

Brush the edge of pastry with the glaze and fold pastry up and around the meat – remember to leave the cutlet bones exposed by folding the pastry underneath. Once you've finished one, repeat for the rest.

Having completed all of the racks, place them on a lined baking tray and bake them in the pre-heated oven for 20-25 minutes, or until golden brown.

Serve with sautéed potatoes and seasonal vegetables or salad.

To find out more about PGI, or for more news, recipes and information, visit EatPGIWelshLamb.com

 25 mins   Serves 8

Ingredients

- 8 x 2 bone mini racks of Welsh Lamb
- 15ml (1 tbsp) oil
- 50g (2oz) button mushrooms, sliced thinly
- 100g (4oz) Ardennes paté
- Seasoning
- 2 x 500g pre-made packet puff pastry
- Egg and milk glaze

WELSH LAMB
CIG OEN CYMRU

It's all about quality time

CRANBERRY &
PISTACHIO NUT ROAST

CRANBERRY & PISTACHIO NUT ROAST

This is a twist on a classic vegetarian Christmas nut roast, with a mushroom risotto base and sticky cranberry top.
Recipe by Anna Jones
Serves 8–10

- A small handful of dried porcini
- 2 tbsp olive oil
- 2 celery stalks, finely chopped
- 2 red onions, finely chopped
- 2 garlic cloves, finely chopped
- 150g risotto rice or pearl barley
- 100ml white wine
- 500ml hot vegetable stock
- 200g mixed wild mushrooms
- 100g pistachios, toasted
- 100g almonds, toasted
- A handful of breadcrumbs from sourdough or ciabatta
- 125g vegetarian cheddar, grated
- 1 red chilli, finely chopped
- 2 eggs, beaten
- 2 sprigs each of sage, rosemary and thyme, leaves picked and chopped
- Zest of 1 lemon
- 2 tbsp soft light brown sugar
- 200g fresh cranberries

1 Start by making the risotto base. Soak the dried porcini in a little boiling water and set aside. Meanwhile, heat the olive oil in a large pan over a low heat. Add the celery and onion and cook for about 10 minutes, until soft and sweet. Add the garlic and cook for another minute.
2 Turn up the heat and add the rice. Cook for a minute or so until you hear it pop, then add the wine and stir till absorbed.
3 Drain the porcini, sieve the liquid and add to the risotto pan, stirring until absorbed. Chop up the porcini and add.
4 Add the hot stock, a ladleful at a time, stirring each one in until it has been completely absorbed, about 20 minutes. Stir as much as you can – this is what will make it creamy. Once the rice is al dente set aside in a bowl to cool.
5 Preheat the oven to 190C/gas 5. Fry the wild mushrooms in a little oil over a medium heat for 5–10 minutes, until starting to crisp. Bash the nuts coarsely, or quickly pulse in a food processor.
6 Once the risotto has cooled, add all other ingredients except the sugar and cranberries. Season, then mix well.
7 Butter a 20cm loaf tin and line the bottom with baking paper. Cook the sugar and cranberries in a pan over a medium heat for 1–2 minutes, then tip into the tin and spread evenly. Pile on the nut roast mixture and pack it down.
8 Cover the loaf with foil and bake for 45 minutes, then remove the foil and cook for a further 15 minutes. Once golden brown on top, remove from the oven and leave to rest for 10 minutes.
9 Use a knife to loosen the tin, then place a serving platter or board on top. Cover your hand with a tea towel, flip the whole lot over, then gently lift the tin off.

....

GRILLED RADICCHIO WITH GORGONZOLA

Serves 6 as a side

- Extra-virgin olive oil
- 1 red onion, finely sliced
- 4 tbsp raisins
- 1 tbsp red wine vinegar
- 100g gorgonzola, plus extra to serve
- Juice of ½ lemon
- 3 heads of radicchio, trimmed and outer leaves removed
- 2 tbsp pine nuts, toasted
- A handful of rocket leaves, to serve

1 Heat a griddle pan over a high heat until scorching hot. Meanwhile, heat a little olive oil in a nonstick frying pan over a medium-low heat. Add the onion and sauté for 10 minutes until soft but not coloured. Add the raisins and cook, stirring, for 1–2 minutes, then add the vinegar and take the pan off the heat.
2 Blitz the cheese, lemon juice, a glug of olive oil and a splash of water in a food processor to form a creamy dressing.
3 Cut the radicchio into 3cm wedges and cook, cut-side down, on the hot griddle pan for a few minutes each side. Remove to a bowl, add the onion mixture and the toasted pine nuts, and toss to combine. Transfer to a serving bowl and drizzle over the gorgonzola dressing. Scatter over the rocket, and crumble over extra gorgonzola to serve, if you like.

RADICCHIO, or Italian red chicory, is a great addition to winter salads, adding a lovely natural spice. Grill or roast radicchio to soften its bitterness, and pair it with pork, pasta and piquant cheeses

GRILLED RADICCHIO WITH GORGONZOLA

CARROTS ROASTED WITH CUMIN SEEDS

TOMATOEY BUTTER BEANS

CARROTS ROASTED WITH CUMIN SEEDS

Serves 6

- 1kg carrots, sliced into 5cm sticks
- 1 tbsp cumin seeds
- 2 tbsp olive oil
- Juice of ½ lemon
- A small bunch of flat-leaf parsley, leaves picked, roughly chopped

1 Preheat the oven to 190C/gas 5. Add the carrots to a pan of boiling water, parboil them for 5 minutes, then drain.
2 Toast the cumin seeds in a dry pan over a medium heat until they start to pop. Toss them with the carrots, the olive oil, a good pinch each of salt and pepper, then transfer to a roasting dish.
3 Pop the dish in the hot oven and roast for 25-35 minutes, until the carrots are browned at the edges, tossing the whole lot halfway through the cooking time. Finish with a squeeze of lemon juice, the chopped parsley, and generous pinch of cracked black pepper.

TOMATOEY BUTTER BEANS

This is quick and easy comfort food, great with some crusty bread. You could even stir in some fried chorizo or bacon at the end if you fancy it.
Serves 2 as a main or 4 as a side

- 2 tbsp olive oil
- 1 large onion, sliced
- 2 garlic cloves, crushed
- 1 tbsp tomato purée
- 800g tinned butter beans, drained and rinsed
- 400g tinned chopped tomatoes
- Crusty bread or toast, to serve

1 Heat the oil in a pan over a gentle heat. Add the onion and garlic, and cook for about 10 minutes, until very soft and starting to turn golden. Add the tomato purée, butter beans and tinned tomatoes, and season well.
2 Simmer for about 20 minutes, adding a little water if it gets too dry. Spoon into a bowl and serve hot, with slices of crusty bread or toast on the side.

CELERY ALLA PARMIGIANA

Let celery take centre stage with this delicious layered vegetable bake.
Serves 6

- 4 celery hearts, bases trimmed
- Extra-virgin olive oil
- 1 small white onion, sliced lengthways
- 3 rashers of pancetta or streaky bacon, chopped
- 2 garlic cloves, chopped
- ½ tsp fennel seeds
- 400g tinned chopped tomatoes
- 1 tbsp chopped thyme leaves
- 75g parmesan, grated

1 Preheat the oven to 180C/gas 4. Use a sharp knife or speed peeler to peel the outer stalks of the celery heart, but keep each heart in 1 piece. Trim the ends to 12-15cm long, cut the celery lengthways into quarters, then across in half.
2 Heat some oil in a pan over a medium heat, and cook the onion and the pancetta or bacon for a few minutes, until the onion is soft. Add the celery and cook, with the lid on, until soft.
3 Meanwhile, heat another pan and add a splash of oil. Add the garlic and fennel seeds, then, when the garlic is golden brown, tip in the tomatoes. Fill the tomato tin with water and pour it in, then season with salt and pepper. Cook the sauce over a medium heat for half an hour or so, until reduced and thick.
4 Remove the lid on the celery pan and let the ingredients brown slightly on the bottom. Lightly oil a 20cm x 20cm baking dish and spoon a little tomato sauce in the bottom. Spread it out and top with a third of the celery. Cover with more sauce, some thyme leaves and a good sprinkle of parmesan. Continue layering, finishing with the last of the tomato sauce, lots of cheese and some salt and pepper. Bake for about 20 minutes, or until heated through and crisp on top.

CELERY ALLA PARMIGIANA

POMEGRANATE This ruby red fruit is native to Iran. Packed with sweet seeds, and rich in vitamins and nutrients, it's not only tasty, but super good for you, too

WINTER SALAD

POTATOES YIACHNI

WINTER SALAD
Serves 6

- 4 small beetroots (preferably different colours), scrubbed and cut into chunks
- 4 carrots, cut into long halves
- 1 red onion, cut into wedges
- 2 tsp coriander seeds
- 150g leftover roast chicken or 100g crumbly cheese, such as feta or white stilton
- ⅓ ciabatta loaf
- A small handful of pumpkin or sunflower seeds
- 1 small pomegranate, halved
- A handful of rocket

Orange & honey dressing
- 1 large orange, peeled and halved
- 2 tbsp honey
- Olive oil

1 Preheat the oven to 190C/gas 5. Place the chopped beetroot, carrot and onion in a roasting pan and set aside.
2 For the dressing, remove the pith from the orange, then carefully slice one half into thin rounds and set aside. Squeeze the other half into a clean jar. Add the honey to the jar and top up with twice the amount of olive oil. Pop the lid on and shake the dressing well.
3 Bash the coriander seeds in a pestle and mortar. Spoon 3 tablespoons of dressing over the vegetables (reserving the rest). Season with salt, pepper and the coriander seeds then toss to coat. Bake for 30-40 minutes, turning the veg halfway through, for even cooking.
4 Meanwhile, tear the chicken into strips or crumble the cheese into chunks, depending which you're using, then tear the bread into large chunks. Place the bread in a mixing bowl and drizzle with a little olive oil. Add to the roasting pan for the last 15 minutes of cooking.

5 Place the seeds on a baking tray in the oven for 2-4 minutes, or until browned and fragrant. Put in a bowl.
6 Hold the pomegranate halves over the bowl and whack the backs (skin side), so the seeds land in the bowl.
7 When the veg is soft in the middle and the ciabatta crisp, remove from the oven and leave to cool slightly in the tray, then tip onto a serving plate. Drizzle a little dressing over the rocket and scatter it over the veg with the chicken or cheese, and orange slices. Serve topped with the seeds and any remaining dressing.

....

POTATOES YIACHNI
Bring a little Mediterranean sun into your winter with a flavour medley of tomato, feta, olive and oregano.
Serves 4

- 4 tbsp olive oil, plus extra to serve
- 1 onion, sliced
- 1 tsp dried oregano, plus a little extra to serve
- 3 garlic cloves, thinly sliced
- 750g all-rounder potatoes, quartered
- 4 tomatoes, quartered, or 400g tinned plum tomatoes
- 3 bay leaves
- 1 tbsp tomato purée
- 200g stoned kalamata olives
- Feta, to serve

1 Heat the oil in a large saucepan over a medium heat and sauté the onion, oregano and garlic for 4-5 minutes, until softened. Season generously.
2 Add the potatoes, tomatoes, bay leaves and tomato purée to the pan and stir well. Add enough water to just cover the mixture and then simmer, covered, over a low heat for 20-30 minutes.
3 Remove the lid, add the kalamata olives and continue to cook, stirring occasionally, for 10 minutes, or until the sauce has thickened and the potatoes are tender. Serve hot with a slab of feta and a sprinkling of oregano and oil, or as a side to grilled poultry.

RABBIT & LEEK LASAGNE

RABBIT & LEEK LASAGNE

Cooking rabbit in this way is really simple, but incredibly rewarding. Use chicken if you prefer, but rabbit is a complete joy to eat.

Serves 8-12

- Olive oil
- 2 garlic cloves, finely sliced
- 4 leeks, sliced into 1cm rounds
- ½ bunch of thyme, leaves picked
- 1 whole tame rabbit, skinned and jointed into 8 pieces
- Flour, for coating
- 375ml white wine
- 750ml-1 litre chicken stock
- 200g white mushrooms, sliced
- 100g parmesan, grated
- 500-600g fresh egg pasta sheets, cut into 20cm x 10cm sheets
- 100g crème fraîche
- 50g fresh breadcrumbs

1 Heat a little oil in a large saucepan and fry the garlic over a medium heat for 1 minute, or until golden. Add the leeks and most of the thyme, reduce the heat and fry for 10-15 minutes, or until the leeks are soft and sticky. Add a splash of water if they start to catch. Remove from the pan and set aside.
2 Add another drizzle of olive oil to the pan. Coat the rabbit pieces in flour and seasoning, then add to the pan, in batches if necessary, and fry for a few minutes, until lightly browned. Return the leeks to the pan, pour in the wine and add enough stock to cover the meat. Bring to the boil over a high heat, then cover and cook over a low heat for around 2 hours, or until the meat is tender and falling off the bone.
3 Remove the rabbit from the pan and shred the meat (discard any bones). Bring the cooking liquid back to the boil and let it simmer for 10 minutes, or until thickened. Stir in the mushrooms and most of the parmesan, season to taste, and simmer for a few more minutes.
4 Preheat the oven to 180C/gas 4.

Lightly oil a large baking dish (roughly 35cm x 25cm). Bring a large pan of salted water to the boil and cook the pasta, in batches, for 1 minute or so. Remove with tongs and drain on a tea towel.
5 Place 1 layer of pasta over the base of the dish. Scatter over a quarter of the meat, then top with a quarter of the sauce. Repeat, finishing with a layer of pasta. Mix the remaining parmesan with the crème fraîche and spread over the lasagne. Toss the breadcrumbs with the remaining thyme and a splash of oil, and scatter on top. Bake for 30 minutes, or until golden and bubbling at the edges. Let stand for 5 minutes before serving.

STROZZAPRETI WITH WALNUT PESTO, SALAMI & RADICCHIO

Serves 4

- 400g strozzapreti pasta
- 8 slices of fennel salami, sliced into strips (see note)
- 1 head of radicchio, shredded

Walnut pesto

- 100g walnuts
- 1 garlic clove
- ½ bunch of marjoram, leaves picked
- A small bunch of parsley, leaves picked
- 80ml-120ml extra-virgin olive oil
- 30g pecorino, grated, plus extra to serve

1 First make your pesto. Toast the walnuts in a dry pan for a few minutes, until golden. Bash the garlic and a pinch of salt with a pestle and mortar, add the walnuts and bash to get a thick paste.
2 Add the herbs and bash again. Drizzle in the oil, and mix into a deep green slick. Stir in the pecorino, and season to taste.
3 Cook the strozzapreti in salted boiling water according to packet instructions.
4 Meanwhile, heat a frying pan until hot and fry the salami until crisp. Drain the pasta, reserving a little of the cooking water for later, then return the pasta to the pan and add the pesto, stirring well. Add enough cooking water to loosen the mixture and make a creamy sauce. Stir in the salami and radicchio and serve with extra pecorino grated over.
Note Fennel salami is available from Waitrose and Italian delis. If unavailable, substitute regular salami.

STROZZAPRETI WITH WALNUT
PESTO, SALAMI & RADICCHIO

STILTON & PEAR GNOCCHI

STILTON & PEAR GNOCCHI

Serves 2
- A knob of butter
- 1 garlic clove, finely sliced
- 1 large pear, peeled, cored and cut into 2cm slices
- 2 tbsp crème fraîche
- 50g leftover stilton
- 400g gnocchi
- Chopped parsley leaves, to serve

1 Bring a large pan of salted water to the boil. Meanwhile, melt the butter in a large pan over a medium heat and add the garlic. Once lightly golden, add the pear and reduce the heat. Cook for 3-4 minutes until softened slightly, then add the crème fraîche and stilton. Heat until the cheese melts.
2 Meanwhile, add the gnocchi to the boiling water and cook for 2 minutes. They're done when they rise to the surface; use a slotted spoon to transfer to the frying pan. Add enough cooking water to loosen the sauce. Toss to coat, season well, add the parsley and serve.

RICOTTA & KALE FLATBREADS

Recipe by Maria Helm Sinksey
Makes 4 pizzas
- Extra-virgin olive oil
- 1 large bunch (or 200g bag) of kale or cavolo nero, leaves finely sliced
- 240ml tomato passata
- 120g ricotta
- 125g fresh mozzarella
- 50g parmesan, finely grated
- Chilli flakes, optional

Pizza dough
- 300ml warm water
- 7g sachet of dry yeast
- 1 tsp sugar
- 500g flour
- 2 tsp fine sea salt
- 2 tbsp extra-virgin olive oil, plus extra to drizzle
- 50g semolina flour

1 Heat a large saucepan over a medium-high heat. Add 1 tablespoon of olive oil, then the kale and sauté until wilted, season to taste, and set aside.
2 To make the pizza dough, pour 125ml of the water into a small bowl. Sprinkle the yeast over the water, leave to activate for a few minutes, then whisk together until smooth. Whisk in the sugar to dissolve, then add 50g of the flour to make a paste. Cover the bowl with clingfilm or a damp towel and let sit for 20 minutes until the mixture bubbles.
3 Combine 400g of the flour with the salt in the bowl of a stand mixer. Reserve the remaining 50g flour to add to the dough if needed. Add the yeast mixture, the remaining water and the olive oil. Use a dough hook to knead the dough for about 10 minutes, until smooth and elastic. Add more flour if the dough is too wet. It should be moist and pliable but not stick to your hands.
4 Place the finished dough in a lightly oiled bowl. Flip it over to coat all sides with oil. Cover the bowl with clingfilm and leave to rise in a warm place, for 1-1½ hours, until doubled in size.
5 Punch the dough down and divide into 4 equal pieces. Roll each piece into a ball and place on a lightly floured plate. Cover the balls with clingfilm and allow to rest for 15 minutes.
6 Separate the dough balls and place them on a lightly floured board. Using your hand or a rolling pin, press each dough ball into a flat patty, then roll into a 0.5cm-thick circle, about 25cm in diameter. Prick the dough all over with a fork and transfer to a baking sheet lightly sprinkled with the semolina flour.
7 Preheat the oven to 230C/gas 8. Top each of the dough rounds with a quarter of the passata and the ricotta. Top with some kale, then some mozzarella and the parmesan. Sprinkle with a pinch of chilli flakes, if you like a bit of heat!
8 Drizzle the pizzas lightly with olive oil, and season with a pinch of salt. Place in the oven (one by one, or two at a time, switching shelves halfway through). Bake for 10 minutes, until the crust is golden and the cheese is bubbling.
9 Slide each pizza onto a cutting board and cool for 5 minutes before cutting into slices - this prevents the hot cheese from sliding around.

RICOTTA & KALE FLATBREADS

FESTIVE HAM

CHICKEN KEDGEREE

BEEF BRISKET STEW
Serves 10

- 1kg beef brisket, rolled and tied
- 1 garlic bulb, smashed
- 2 red onions, cut into wedges
- 3 celery stalks, cut into chunks
- 4 carrots, cut into chunks
- 1 small squash, flesh cut in chunks
- 800g tinned chopped tomatoes
- 820g tinned chickpeas
- A few thyme or rosemary sprigs
- 2 heaped tsp cumin seeds
- 2 heaped tsp ground coriander
- 1 heaped tsp ground cinnamon
- Olive oil
- Grated zest and juice of 1 lemon
- A small bunch of parsley, chopped
- 600g couscous

1 Preheat the oven to 180C/gas 4. Season the brisket with salt and pepper and place in a large ovenproof casserole pan with a lid. Add the garlic, all the veg, the tinned tomatoes and chickpeas with their liquids, thyme, spices and a drizzle of oil. Mix it up, then roast for 4–5 hours, till the meat is very tender and falling apart. Use 2 forks to shred the meat.
2 Mix the lemon zest with half the parsley and scatter it over the brisket. Add the couscous to a bowl and just cover it with boiling water. Cover with a plate till couscous has absorbed the water. Season, add the lemon juice and remaining parsley, and fluff it up with a fork. Serve with the beef stew.

FESTIVE HAM
Makes 3kg glazed gammon

- 3kg middle gammon joint
- 1 cinnamon stick
- ½ onion
- 6 cloves, plus 2 large handfuls to stud the meat (optional)
- 2 bay leaves
- 10 peppercorns
- Apple juice or water

Glaze

- 200g marmalade
- 2 tbsp soft brown sugar
- 2 tsp wholegrain mustard

1 Preheat the oven to 160C/gas 2½. Place the gammon in a large pan with the cinnamon, onion, cloves, bay leaves and peppercorns. Half-fill the pan with apple juice or water, cover with foil and cook in the oven for 45–60 minutes. The gammon is done when a skewer inserted in the centre is warm to the touch. Leave the joint to cool, covered, for 30 minutes.
2 Remove the skin, leaving a good amount of fat. Score the fat criss-cross style, without cutting through to the flesh; stud with cloves, if you like.
3 For the glaze, preheat the oven to 160C/gas 2½. Place all the ingredients in a small pan over a medium heat and stir until the mixture is warmed through. Brush the glaze over the cooked joint, making sure that the fat is well covered, and roast in the oven for 30–40 minutes.
4 Keep basting the meat with the glaze every few minutes until it's all used up. Rest the gammon before carving.

CHICKEN KEDGEREE
Serves 4

- 25g butter
- 2 tbsp olive oil
- 1 onion, finely chopped
- 1 garlic clove, crushed
- 2 tsp medium curry powder
- 300g cooked basmati rice (approx 200g raw)
- 200g cooked chicken, shredded
- Zest of 1 lemon
- 4 boiled eggs, each cut into 8 wedges
- Small bunch of dill, finely chopped

1 Heat the butter and oil in a sauté pan over a medium heat, then fry the onion until soft and translucent (about 10 minutes). Add the garlic and cook for 1 minute, then stir in the curry powder. Cook for 1 minute, then add the rice. Heat through, stirring well. Add the chicken and zest and heat through for a further 1–2 minutes before adding the eggs and the dill. Season to taste

FAMILY FAVOURITE

CAJUN ROAST CHICKEN, VEG & SPICY GRAVY

CAJUN ROAST CHICKEN, VEG & SPICY GRAVY

Serves 6

- 1 x 1.6kg chicken
- 1 tsp dried oregano
- 2 tsp smoked paprika
- 2 tsp cayenne pepper
- 1 tsp allspice berries
- 1 orange
- 1 bunch of thyme, leaves picked
- Olive oil
- 1 onion, roughly chopped
- 750g carrots, 1 roughly chopped, the rest halved lengthways
- 1.25kg potatoes, cut in half
- 4 garlic cloves, skins on
- 2 tbsp honey
- 1 chicken stock cube
- 1 tbsp flour

1 Preheat the oven to 200C/gas 6. Place the chicken on a clean board. Bash the dry herbs and spices in a pestle and mortar with a good pinch of salt and pepper. Grate in some zest from the orange, add half the thyme, and bash again. Mix in 1 tablespoon of olive oil then rub the spice mix all over the chicken.
2 Place the onion and carrot in a roasting tin. Sit the chicken on top, and drizzle with olive oil. Halve the zested orange; pop 1 half into the chicken's cavity and reserve the other. Put the chicken in the oven and reduce the heat to 180C/gas 4. Roast for 75-80 minutes, till the chicken is golden and when pierced in the thickest part, the juices run clear.
3 Meanwhile, parboil the potatoes for 5-6 minutes; drain in a colander and let them steam dry for a few minutes. Shake the colander to scuff the edges, then tip into a roasting tin and season with salt. Mix in the garlic and a glug of oil. Roast with the chicken for 50 minutes.
4 Meanwhile, parboil the carrots for 4 minutes; drain and steam dry. Tip into a roasting tin, season, and mix with the honey, remaining thyme and orange juice and a drizzle of olive oil. Set aside.
5 When the chicken is cooked, remove it from the oven and set aside. Pop the carrots into the oven and check the potatoes, shaking the tray to turn them, then turn the oven up to 200C/gas 6. Keep an eye on the veg so they don't burn, while you make the gravy.

PORK, SAGE & APPLE STUFFING

6 Transfer the chicken to a board to rest and loosely cover in foil. Dissolve the stock cube in 750ml just-boiled water. Place the roasting tin over a medium heat. Sprinkle in the flour and scrape the sticky bits off the bottom. Get the flour nice and dark (not burnt), then add the stock. Bring to the boil then simmer rapidly for 5 minutes, stirring. When the gravy reaches the consistency you like, strain it through a sieve. By now the roast veg should be ready to serve with the cajun roast chicken and spicy gravy.

PORK, SAGE & APPLE STUFFING

Serves 12-14, with leftovers

- 50g butter
- 50ml olive oil
- 2 onions, diced
- 2 celery stalks, finely diced
- 2 garlic cloves, finely chopped
- 2 large bramley apples, peeled, cored and diced
- A bunch of sage, leaves picked and chopped
- ½ bunch of parsley, leaves picked and chopped
- 850g best-quality pork sausage meat
- 280g breadcrumbs
- 1 egg, beaten

1 Melt the butter with the oil in a wide pan over a medium heat, then add the onion, celery and garlic and cook, stirring occasionally, for 5-8 minutes, till the veg is soft but not coloured. Add the apple, cover, and cook for 4-5 minutes, until starting to soften. Move to a tray to cool.
2 Once cooled, tip into a large bowl, add the rest of the ingredients and use your hands to scrunch everything together.
3 Stuff the neck cavity of the turkey and put the rest of the stuffing in a greased baking dish. Cover with foil and bake for the last 45 minutes of the bird's cooking time. While the bird is resting, remove the foil from the dish; cook for a further 15-20 minutes, till golden.

LEEK, BACON & CHEESE BAKE

HAM & PEAS
Serves 6-8

- 3 ham hocks (roughly 2.3kg in total)
- 2 leeks, trimmed
- 1 celery stalk, trimmed
- 3 carrots
- Olive oil
- 2 bay leaves
- 100g pearl barley
- 1 litre chicken stock
- 400g frozen peas
- 1 small bunch of curly parsley, leaves finely chopped
- 1 heaped tbsp mint sauce
- A loaf of bread and English mustard, to serve

1 The day before you want to cook this recipe, prepare the hocks by soaking them in a pot of cold water overnight. The next day, drain the hocks, refill the pot with fresh cold water and bring it to the boil. Discard the salty water, rinse the hocks, and repeat once more.
2 Finely slice the leeks, celery and carrots using a food processor or mandolin. Add the vegetables to a large pan with a glug of olive oil, a pinch of salt and pepper, and the bay leaves. Sweat over a medium heat, stirring occasionally, for 15 minutes until the vegetables are soft but not coloured.
3 Add the drained ham hocks, pearl barley and chicken stock. Bring to the boil then cook, with the lid on, over a medium-low heat for 3 hours or until the meat is very tender. Check on it occasionally, and top up with more hot stock or water if it gets too dry.
4 Using tongs, transfer the ham hocks to a clean board and carefully remove all the fat and bones. Shred the meat then add it to the broth. Turn the heat up and add the peas. When they're tender, stir the parsley and mint sauce into the broth. Serve with slices of bread and some good English mustard.

LEEK, BACON & CHEESE BAKE
This bake makes a lovely light meal on its own, or as a side dish to steak, or roast chicken with salad greens.
Serves 2 as a main, 4 as a side

- Olive oil
- 6 rashers of smoked streaky bacon, chopped
- 400g leeks, sliced
- 250ml vegetable stock
- 2 tsp wholegrain mustard
- 2 tbsp crème fraîche
- 60g grated cheddar cheese
- 2 big handfuls of breadcrumbs

1 Preheat the oven to 190C/gas 5. Heat a little olive oil in a saucepan and fry the bacon until it begins to colour, then add the leeks and continue to cook until softened. Add the vegetable stock and mustard, season with pepper, to taste. Cover the pan with a lid and cook for a further 5-10 minutes, then remove from the heat and stir in the crème fraîche and most of the cheese.
2 Tip everything into a baking dish and top with the breadcrumbs and the remaining cheese. Drizzle with a little more olive oil and bake for 20 minutes until golden and bubbling.

LEEKS A mild, sweet member of the onion family, the leek's flavour and versatility makes it a winter favourite, used regularly in tasty stews, soups, sauces and gratins

HAM & PEAS

ALL-IN PIE

Pies are perfect for turning leftovers into a meal - get everything in a dish with a bit of liquid for gravy. This pastry lid is made with suet, so it's extra crisp; to make life easier, use readymade shortcrust or puff pastry.
Serves 8

- 500g (or however much you have) cooked ham or turkey, shredded
- 1 heaped tbsp seasoned flour
- Olive oil
- 2-3 garlic cloves, sliced
- A few sage sprigs, leaves picked and shredded
- 500g leftover veg, cut into large, even-sized chunks
- 300ml ale
- 300ml chicken stock
- 100g cheddar, crumbled into pieces

Pastry
- 250g flour
- ½ tsp baking powder
- 125g suet
- 1 egg, beaten with a little milk

1 For the pastry, put the flour in a bowl with the baking powder, suet and a good pinch of salt. Gradually pour in 150ml water to combine; if it's a little dry, add a splash more. Bring the pastry together and wrap in clingfilm. Chill in the fridge for at least 30 minutes.
2 Toss the meat in the seasoned flour. Add a glug of oil to a large saucepan, add the garlic and cook over a medium heat until golden. Add the sage and meat and cook for 5 minutes, stirring occasionally. Add the veg, toss to coat, then pour in the ale and stock. Bring to the boil, then reduce the heat and simmer for around 15 minutes; you just need to reduce the gravy to give it good flavour.
3 Preheat the oven to 180C/gas 4. When the filling is ready, ladle half of it into a pie dish and dot over half the cheese; top with the remaining of the filling and cheese. Remove your pastry from the fridge and roll out to 5mm thick, or large enough to fit the shape of your pie dish. Brush the rim of the dish with a little beaten egg. Drape the pastry over the dish; trim any excess. Crimp the edges and brush the top with more egg wash. Make an incision in the middle for the steam to escape and bake for 30 minutes, until golden.

VENISON & CHESTNUT RAGÙ

VENISON & CHESTNUT RAGÙ

This rich, mouthwatering ragù is packed with fragrant flavours. Best served piping hot over your favourite fresh pasta, with plenty of parmesan.
Serves 6-8

- 1 carrot, roughly chopped
- 2 celery stalks, roughly chopped
- 1 large red onion, roughly chopped
- 75g butter
- 3 bay leaves
- 1 small cinnamon stick
- 500g minced venison
- 200g vacuum-packed chestnuts, roughly chopped
- A grating of nutmeg
- 1 tsp tomato purée
- A glass of red wine
- 1 litre chicken stock
- 1 small bunch of parsley, chopped
- Fresh pasta and parmesan, to serve

1 For the ragù, finely chop the carrot, celery and onion in a food processor.

2 Melt 25g butter in a large saucepan over a medium heat. Add the chopped vegetables, bay leaves and cinnamon. Gently cook, covered, for 10 minutes or until the veg are soft and sweet but not coloured. Add the venison and stir into the vegetables, breaking up any lumps with a wooden spoon. As the meat releases its juices, keep stirring and frying until they have evaporated. Add half the remaining butter, the chestnuts and a grating of nutmeg, and cook for 15-20 minutes until the veg have started to caramelise and the venison is cooked.
2 Stir in the purée, then after a minute or so add the wine. Stir and scrape up all the sticky bits from the bottom of the pan. When the wine has bubbled away, add the stock, bring to the boil then simmer gently for about 30 minutes, stirring occasionally. Once the liquid has reduced slightly and you have a hearty sauce, turn off the heat and season to taste. Serve with fresh pasta, and top with parsley and grated parmesan.

ST EMILION AU CHOCOLAT

ST EMILION AU CHOCOLAT

Recipe by Jeremy Lee

Jeremy Lee, chef at Quo Vadis, stays true to the dessert recipe championed by British cookery icon Elizabeth David. He makes large cakes of this at the restaurant, but suggests serving in your prettiest cups at home.

Fills 8 pretty cups

- 16 almond macaroons (see note)
- A good measure (30–60ml) of quaffing cognac
- 110g butter, softened
- 110g sugar
- 200ml milk
- 225g dark chocolate (70%-cocoa), broken into pieces
- 1 egg yolk

1 Set aside 8 pretty cups or ramekins. Gently render the macaroons into small pieces and divvy them up between the 8 cups, leaving a few large crumbs for sprinkling over the top at the end. Add a jigger of cognac to each cup (we confess to liking a fair whack).
2 In a bowl, beat the butter and sugar together with gusto, until pale and fluffy, then set aside.
3 Pour the milk into a saucepan and bring it to a gentle simmer. Place the pieces of chocolate in a bowl, pour over the warm milk and beat it thoroughly, until all of the chocolate is melted.
4 Gently beat the egg yolk into the creamed butter and sugar. Slowly add the chocolate mixture and carefully mix it all together until well combined. Pour into the cups, strew the leftover macaroon crumbs on top and dampen each cup with a tiny tot more of cognac. Leave the desserts to cool to room temperature, then place in the fridge overnight to set. Remove the pots from the fridge 15 minutes before serving.
Note You will need French-style macaroons for this. Buy from food halls, French bakeries or online. If unavailable, you can substitute with amaretti.

MINCE PIE COOKIES

MINCE PIE COOKIES

Leftover Christmas mincemeat is a perfect excuse for making these tasty little treats, great for the holidays.

Makes 30 cookies

- 250g unsalted butter, softened
- 140g sugar
- 1 egg yolk
- Grated zest of 1 clementine
- 300g flour
- 1 x 411g jar fruit mincemeat

1 Preheat the oven to 180C/gas 4 and line 2 baking trays with baking paper. Beat the butter and sugar together in a large bowl until creamy. Add the egg yolk and clementine zest and beat again to combine. Sift in the flour then fold through most of the mincemeat and stir until the mixture comes together.
2 Pull off little biscuit-sized clumps of dough, space them evenly over the trays and gently press down slightly to shape into cookies. Dot a little of your saved mincemeat on top of each cookie to make them look extra delicious. Pop them in the oven for 10 minutes, or till golden but still a bit doughy in the middle.
3 Serve warm, or turn onto a wire rack to cool, then store in an airtight container.
4 If you don't want to bake the whole batch, shape the dough into biscuits then freeze. Alternatively, shape into a log and slice off rounds as you want to bake them. Just pop in the oven at 180C/ gas 4 for 10–15 minutes until golden.

BOOZY BANANA SPLIT

BOOZY BANANA SPLIT
Serves 6
- 40g pecan nuts, roughly crushed
- ½ tbsp icing sugar
- 1 tbsp unsalted butter
- 2 tbsp dark muscovado sugar
- 6 small bananas (not too ripe), peeled and halved lengthways
- 50ml golden rum
- 6 scoops of rum and raisin ice cream
- 100ml double cream, whipped
- 2 tbsp good-quality chocolate sauce
- 3 glacé cherries, roughly chopped

1 Toast the pecans in a pan over a low heat for 2–3 minutes, then combine in a bowl with the icing sugar. Set aside.
2 Heat the butter and muscovado sugar in a large pan over a medium heat for 2–3 minutes, stirring constantly. Add the bananas and cook for 3–5 minutes, or until soft, turning once halfway through. Add the rum to the pan, and carefully set alight to flambé the bananas. Once the flames have died down and the alcohol has burnt off, the bananas are ready.
3 To serve, divide the bananas between 6 plates and top each one with a scoop of rum and raisin ice cream, a spoonful of whipped cream, a drizzle of chocolate sauce, some chopped cherries and sprinkle over the toasted pecans.

RUM BABAS WITH CHANTILLY CREAM
Serves 12
- 430g flour
- 30g granulated sugar
- 10g fast-action yeast
- 4 eggs, beaten
- 2 tsp grated orange zest
- 225g unsalted butter, diced and softened, plus a little for greasing
- 30g currants

Rum syrup
- 240g caster sugar
- 1 vanilla pod, split lengthways, seeds scraped and kept for chantilly cream
- 360ml dark rum

Chantilly cream
- 300ml cream
- Seeds of 1 vanilla pod
- 20g icing sugar
- A splash of dark rum

1 Whisk the flour, sugar, yeast and a pinch of salt together in a bowl.
2 Place the eggs, zest and 100ml cold water in the bowl of an electric mixer and beat until combined. With the mixer on a low speed, gradually add the flour mixture and mix until a loose dough forms, about 2 minutes.
3 Add the softened butter, a piece at a time, and mix for 2 minutes, then add the currants and mix till combined.
4 Thoroughly grease twelve 125ml dariole moulds with the extra butter. Pour in the batter so that each mould is about halfway full then cover with a tea towel and leave to rise for 2 hours at room temperature, or until the batter is just rising above the moulds.
5 Meanwhile, preheat the oven to 180C/gas 4. Once the batter has risen, pop the moulds in the oven and bake for about 30 minutes, until golden brown. Allow to cool in the moulds for 5 minutes then turn onto a wire rack to cool completely. (If making ahead, store in an airtight container for up to 3 days, until needed.)
6 To make the rum syrup, place the caster sugar, vanilla pod (not the seeds) and 600ml water in a saucepan and bring to a simmer over a medium heat, stirring constantly. Add the rum and simmer for 3 minutes more, then turn off the heat.
7 Using tongs, carefully place each baba in the syrup. Leave to soak for at least 10 minutes, turning to make sure all sides are soaked through.
8 For the chantilly cream, beat all the ingredients together with an electric whisk or mixer until soft peaks form.
9 Using a slotted spoon, lift the babas from the syrup, and place on a serving dish or in bowls. Drizzle with extra syrup and serve with chantilly cream.

RUM BABAS WITH CHANTILLY CREAM

GROWN-UP
TREAT

EASY &
ELEGANT

SPICED APPLE CHRISTMAS CAKE

CITRUS-POACHED PEARS

GINGER & ORANGE SYLLABUBS WITH FIGS

Serves 12

- 4 tbsp sugar
- 2 balls of stem ginger, finely chopped, plus 3 tbsp syrup from the jar
- 120ml chilled sweet white wine or prosecco
- Zest of 4 clementines and juice of 3
- 3 figs, halved
- 300ml double cream

1 In a bowl, combine the sugar, ginger syrup, wine or prosecco and the zest and juice of 2 clementines. Stir until the sugar dissolves then set aside to cool.
2 Preheat the grill to a high heat. Sprinkle the fig halves with the zest and juice of 1 clementine and grill for 7 minutes, or until warmed through. Remove, then halve the figs again.
3 Pour the cream into the reserved syrup and whisk lightly to soft peaks. Spoon the syllabub into small, chilled glasses and top with a fig quarter, chopped ginger and remaining zest.

SPICED APPLE CHRISTMAS CAKE

This is a wonderful, gluten-free treat, made with apples, pine nuts, and plenty of warming Christmas spices.
Serves 12

- 225g butter, room temperature, cut into cubes, plus extra for greasing
- 450g bramley apples, roughly chopped
- 200g medjool dates
- 100g raisins
- 4 eggs, beaten
- 150g gluten-free white bread flour, plus a teaspoon extra
- 100g ground almonds
- 1½ tbsp gluten-free baking powder
- 1 tsp ground cinnamon
- ½ tsp ground ginger
- A good grating of nutmeg
- 2 tbsp pine nuts
- 2 tbsp demerara sugar

1 Preheat the oven to 180C/gas 4. Grease the base of a round 23cm cake tin and line with greaseproof paper. Place the apples in a food processor with the dates, butter and half the raisins and blitz until combined. Using a spatula, scrape into a bowl and mix in a third of the beaten eggs.
2 In a separate bowl combine the flour, almonds, baking powder, cinnamon, ginger and nutmeg. Add a third to the apple mixture and combine, then continue adding and combining the egg and flour mixtures in alternating batches until all mixed together. Finish by folding through the remaining raisins then pour into the prepared cake tin.

3 Combine the pine nuts, demerara sugar and extra teaspoon of gluten-free flour in a bowl and scatter over the cake mixture. Bake for 50–60 minutes, until golden and cooked through. Leave the cake to cool in the tin for 10 minutes before turning out onto a wire rack to cool completely.

CITRUS-POACHED PEARS

Recipe by Anna Hansen
Serves 2

- 2 pears, peeled
- 200g granulated sugar
- Peeled zest and juice of 1 lemon
- Peeled zest and juice of 1 orange
- 1 cinnamon stick (or cloves, allspice, star anise or a combination)
- Double cream, to serve

1 You'll need a saucepan large enough to hold all the pears. Put all the ingredients except the pears and cream into the pan, pour in 500ml water and bring to the boil. When the sugar has dissolved, reduce the heat and carefully lower the pears into the syrup. Simmer gently for 10–12 minutes until the pears are tender, then remove from the heat and leave to cool. Serve the pears with some double cream, and 4 tablespoons of the poaching liquid per person.

DRIED FRUIT SALAD

PINEAPPLE UPSIDE-DOWN CAKE

DRIED FRUIT SALAD

Serves 2

- 150g dried apricots
- 150g dried figs
- 50g dried blueberries
- Juice of 1 orange, zest of half
- 50g pecan nuts
- 2 tbsp Greek-style yoghurt
- A drizzle of honey

1 Roughly chop the apricots and figs and place in a bowl with the blueberries, orange juice and zest. Leave to macerate for 30 minutes. Heat a frying pan and toast the nuts, then remove and set aside. Add the fruit to the pan and heat through. Mix the nuts back in and serve with the yoghurt and honey.

PINEAPPLE UPSIDE-DOWN CAKE

Serves 6

- 25g butter, for greasing
- 50g demerara sugar
- 4 tinned pineapple rings, in syrup
- 6 glacé cherries
- 50g butter
- 50g caster sugar
- 1 large egg
- 65g self-raising flour
- 15g semolina
- 1-2 tbsp milk

1 Preheat the oven to 190C/gas 5. Grease an 18cm sandwich tin lightly around the sides; thicker on the base. Sprinkle with the demerara sugar and arrange the fruit in the bottom of the tin.
2 Beat the butter, caster sugar, egg, flour and semolina in a bowl till smooth, adding enough milk to make a soft, dropping consistency.
3 Spread the batter over the fruit in the tin, and smooth it level. Bake in the centre of the oven for 30-35 minutes until the top is firm and the cake is shrinking from the sides of the tin.
4 Remove from the oven, wait for 2-3 minutes, then invert onto a warm plate, leaving the tin in place for a few minutes.
5 For a glaze, heat some pineapple syrup in a pan until thickened. Remove the tin, brush the cake with glaze; serve warm.

CHRISTMAS CAKE TRUFFLES

Turn those Christmas leftovers into the ultimate, spoil-yourself treat.
Serves 25-30

- A large slice of leftover Christmas cake or a large handful of cake crumbs
- 250g 70%-cocoa chocolate, chopped
- 300ml double cream
- A knob of butter
- 25ml brandy or other booze
- 100g mixed nuts, toasted

1 Blitz the cake and chocolate in a food processor until you get coarse crumbs, then tip into a large bowl. Gently heat the cream in a pan over a low heat; you don't want it to boil, so turn off before it starts bubbling. Add the butter, stir until melted, then pour over the cake mixture and stir. Add the brandy and a pinch of salt and stir till combined. Leave to cool, then refrigerate for 1-2 hours to firm up.
2 Blitz the nuts in a food processor until finely ground and pour onto a plate.
3 Remove the chocolate mixture from the fridge 5 minutes before you want to make your truffles. Using a teaspoon and clean hands, form small balls of the mixture and gently - but quickly - roll them in the nuts. Pop onto a lined baking tray and refrigerate for 30 minutes to firm up. These will keep in the fridge in an airtight container for a few days.

CHRISTMAS CAKE TRUFFLES

CITRUS & ALMOND POLENTA CAKE

MARMALADE CAKE

This is the easiest winter cake ever, full of warming, zesty goodness!
Serves 10

- 200g butter softened, plus a large knob for greasing
- 4 tbsp demerara sugar
- 2 small oranges, thinly sliced
- 200g golden caster sugar
- 6 heaped tbsp fine-cut marmalade
- 4 large eggs, beaten
- 200g self-raising flour
- 50g ground almonds
- Grated zest and juice of 2 oranges

1 Preheat the oven to 180C/gas 4. Grease the base and sides of a 23cm loose-bottomed cake tin. Sprinkle the base with demerara sugar and layer the orange slices on top, slightly overlapping.
2 Cream the butter and caster sugar until pale and fluffy, then beat in half of the marmalade, followed by the beaten eggs. Fold in the flour, ground almonds, orange zest and juice and a pinch of salt.
3 Carefully pour the cake batter into the tin. Place in the oven and bake for about 50 minutes, till golden and firm to touch. Remove from the oven and allow to stand for a few minutes. Very carefully, while it's still slightly warm, turn out the cake onto a serving plate.
4 Prick holes in the cake with a skewer. Make a glaze by warming the rest of the marmalade in a pan with a little water, then spoon over the cake. Serve warm.

CITRUS & ALMOND POLENTA CAKE

This is a flourless cake made with ground almonds and polenta, giving it a gorgeous texture.
Serves 12

- 225g butter, softened, plus extra for greasing
- 225g sugar, plus 2 tbsp
- 3 eggs
- 125g ground almonds
- 125g polenta
- 1 tsp baking powder
- Zest of 2 oranges, 1 grated, 1 in long strips, and juice of 1
- Zest and juice of 2 lemons, plus a little extra juice for the icing
- 75g icing sugar

1 Preheat the oven to 170C/gas 3. Grease and line the base of a 23cm springform tin. Cream the butter and 225g sugar till pale, then beat in the eggs one at a time. Stir in the almonds, polenta, baking powder, orange juice and grated zest, and the lemon zest and juice. Pour into the tin and bake for 50–60 minutes until golden and just firm in the middle. Leave to cool in tin.
2 Meanwhile, bring the remaining sugar and 2 tablespoons of water to boil in a pan. Remove from heat and stir in the orange zest strips. Leave to cool.
3 Sift the icing sugar into a bowl and add the extra lemon juice until you have a thin icing. Drizzle over the cake, drain orange strips and sprinkle on top.

RHUBARB RUMBA

SGROPPINO

HOT SPICED CIDER

RHUBARB RUMBA
Serves 3
- 1 stick of rhubarb
- 1 tsp of sugar
- 30ml rhubarb syrup or cordial
- Prosecco, chilled

1 Preheat the oven to 180C/gas 4 Carefully using a mandolin or peeler, thinly slice the rhubarb lengthways, then place on a baking tray and sprinkle with the sugar. Bake for 10-12 minutes until softened then transfer to a plate and allow to cool.
2 Place 2 rhubarb strips in each glass, cover with syrup or cordial and allow to macerate for a few minutes. Top up each glass with chilled prosecco and serve.

SGROPPINO
Serves 2
- 2 scoops of lemon sorbet
- 120ml prosecco, chilled
- 50ml vodka or limoncello

1 Place the lemon sorbet, prosecco, and the vodka or limoncello in a blender, and briefly pulse until completely combined. Pour into chilled glasses, top up with a splash or two of extra chilled prosecco and serve immediately.

HOT SPICED CIDER
Makes 2 litres
- 2 litres cider
- 1 orange, halved
- 8 cloves
- 1 cinnamon stick
- 1 bay leaf
- ½ nutmeg
- 1 star anise
- 1 tsp allspice

1 Place the cider in a large pan, then stud the orange halves with the cloves. Add to the cider with the other spices. Gently heat for about 20 minutes, without allowing it to boil. Strain and ladle into mugs or heatproof glasses.

PROSECCO Not just for summer, this Italian sparkling wine is a popular party drink any time of year. In winter, mix it with juices or fruit syrups, or make Bellini cocktails by stirring it into glasses with peach purée

Get Jamie

and receive a free copy of Jamie's 15-Minute Meals

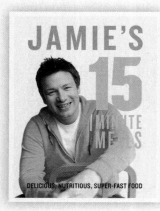

If you've enjoyed these recipes, you might like to know you can subscribe to *Jamie* from just £29.95 a year, saving 25% on the cover price. Not only this, but pay by direct debit and we'll send you a free copy of Jamie's 15-Minute Meals.

APRICOT & GINGER CHUTNEY

BUMBU KACANG

APRICOT & GINGER CHUTNEY

Makes 700ml

- 1 tbsp olive oil
- 1 onion, sliced
- 1 tsp ground cinnamon
- 1 tbsp mustard seeds
- 450g apricots, quartered
- 100g ginger, chopped
- 100g brown sugar
- 200ml white wine vinegar
- 3 tbsp currants

1 Heat the oil in a pan. Soften the onion and add the cinnamon and mustard. Cook a few minutes. Stir in the apricots and ginger. Add the other ingredients. Slowly dissolve the sugar and simmer till the apricots are soft. Store in sterilised jars; it's best left for a month before eating.

STRAWBERRY BALSAMIC VINEGAR

Makes approx 650ml

- 100ml balsamic vinegar
- 450ml white wine vinegar
- 100g sugar
- 500g strawberries

1 Warm the vinegars and sugar in a pan over a low heat until the sugar dissolves. Turn up the heat and bring to the boil. Meanwhile, hull and quarter the strawberries, place in a bowl and mash with a potato masher. Pour over the hot vinegar, allow to cool then steep for 24–48 hours. Pour through a sieve lined with muslin and store in sterilised bottles until ready to use to dress salads (savoury or sweet) or sprinkled over ice cream.

BUMBU KACANG

Our favourite satay sauce is this Indonesian recipe. Not as sweet as the Thai version, but still with a spicy kick, it's a must with chicken skewers, or for marinating meat before grilling.

Makes 400g

- 2 shallots, finely chopped
- Peanut oil or sunflower oil
- 2 lemongrass stalks, tough outer layers removed, white part finely chopped
- 2 garlic cloves, finely chopped
- 3cm piece of ginger, grated
- ½ tsp ground cumin
- ½ tsp ground coriander
- A good pinch of crumbled dried chilli
- 20g tamarind pulp, dissolved in 100ml water for 10 minutes
- 1½ tsp sugar
- 150g peanuts, roasted and ground

1 Gently fry the shallots in a little peanut oil in a frying pan for 5 minutes until soft. Stir in the lemongrass, garlic and ginger. Continue to gently cook for 10 minutes, until fragrant, adding the cumin, coriander and dried chilli for the last 5 minutes. Add the tamarind water to the pan and bring to the boil. Stir in the sugar and ground peanuts then taste for seasoning – it will need a little salt. Stir in a tablespoon of peanut oil and loosen with water until you have your preferred consistency – you may want a thinner sauce if you're using as a marinade.

SALTED CARAMEL

This is brilliant over vanilla ice cream.

Makes about 225g

- 200g sugar
- 75ml double cream
- 50g butter, cubed
- ½ tsp sea salt flakes

1 Place the sugar in a large saucepan with 50ml water. Gently heat on low, carefully swirling the pan but not stirring, until just melted. Turn up the heat a little and simmer gently, swirling regularly, until you have a clear, dark golden caramel. Remove the pan from the heat then carefully and quickly whisk in the cream and butter. It will splutter a bit, so be careful. Keep whisking until smooth, then beat in the salt. Let cool. If making in advance, keep it chilled but bring back to room temperature before using. You can make this up to 2 days in advance.

OREGANO OIL

Blitz in a food processor with the garlic and peppers. Season, add the cheese and mix well, then drizzle in enough oil to give you a loose texture. Keep in a sterilised jar in the fridge, and stir into pasta, or eat on slices of toast.

CORIANDER & ALMOND PASTE

Makes about 350g

- 2 tbsp ghee
- 1 tsp cumin seeds
- 100g almonds
- 2 shallots
- 1 red chilli
- 2 large bunches of coriander
- Juice of 1 lime

1 Melt the ghee in a frying pan and toast the cumin seeds. Add to a blender with the almonds and blitz to a paste. Add the shallots, chilli and coriander and blitz for 1–2 minutes. Season well, add the lime juice, and a splash of water. Pulse to a loose paste, adding water as needed. Keep in a sterilised jar in the fridge.

VEGAN BASIL PESTO

Makes about 125g

- 2 large bunches of basil, leaves picked
- 2 garlic cloves, roughly chopped
- A handful of hazelnuts or pine nuts
- Extra-virgin olive oil

1 Blitz the basil, garlic and nuts in a food processor. Season and mix with enough oil to create a pesto. Keep in a sterilised jar in the fridge.

SUNDRIED TOMATO PASTE

Stir through pasta, or serve on toast, topped with goat's cheese.
Makes about 150g

- 140g drained sundried tomatoes
- 2 garlic cloves, chopped
- A handful of basil leaves
- A pinch of chilli flakes (optional)
- 2 tbsp extra-virgin olive oil

1 Blitz the drained sundried tomatoes in a food processor with remaining ingredients. Keeps in a sterilised jar in the fridge for up to 2 weeks.

OREGANO OIL

This herb oil, which is also lovely made with rosemary, can be drizzled over pizza, foccacia, pasta or vegetables.
Makes 1 litre

- ½ small bunch of oregano
- 5 black peppercorns
- 2 strips of lemon peel
- 1 garlic clove, crushed
- About 1 litre extra-virgin olive oil

1 Put all the ingredients in a sterilised glass bottle, seal, and leave for 2 weeks in a dark place so the flavours can infuse. Drizzle the oil over pizza, pasta or salad.

LEMON PICKLE

Beautiful with a curry.
Makes about 400g

- 8 lemons
- 1 tbsp vegetable oil
- A 3cm-piece of ginger, finely grated
- 2 green chillies, deseeded, finely sliced
- 1 tsp asafoetida
- 2 tsp mustard seeds
- 2 tbsp sugar

1 Cut 4 lemons into 1cm pieces, discarding the seeds. Juice the other lemons. In a pan, heat the oil, then add the ginger, chilli, asafoetida and mustard seeds, and fry for 1 minute. Add the lemons, juice and sugar, and a little water. Cook for 10–15 minutes, till softened, shiny and thick. Season to taste, and serve with curry.

CHARRED RED PEPPER PESTO

Makes about 450g

- ½ bunch of thyme, leaves picked
- A handful of hazelnuts
- 2 garlic cloves, roughly chopped
- 1 x 450g jar roasted peppers, drained
- A handful of grated pecorino
- Extra-virgin olive oil

1 In a small pan, gently toast the thyme and hazelnuts till the nuts start to colour.

CORIANDER & ALMOND PASTE

PESTOS AND PASTES are a seriously easy way to add a burst of herby flavour to dishes, whether spooned over salads, stirred into soups, or simply spread on toast with your choice of toppings

CHIMICHURRI SAUCE

WALNUT & PARSLEY PESTO

WALNUT & PARSLEY PESTO

Brilliant on pasta, crostini, or lamb.
Make about 400g

- 150g walnuts
- 2 garlic cloves, chopped
- A large bunch of parsley, chopped
- 80g parmesan, grated
- About 100ml extra-virgin olive oil
- Lemon juice, to taste

1 Bash the walnuts using a pestle and mortar. Bash in the garlic well, then the parsley. (You could also use a blender.) Stir in the cheese, then the oil. Season with lemon juice and black pepper.

ROMESCO SAUCE

This pairs well with grilled food, especially chicken and seafood. Look for nora chillies in Spanish delis or thetapaslunchcompany.co.uk.
Makes about 420g

- 6 dried nora chillies, or 1 tsp each of sweet and smoked paprika
- 1 red pepper
- Olive oil
- 1 slice of bread
- ½ onion, chopped
- 1 tomato, peeled, seeded and chopped
- 1 garlic clove
- 50g blanched almonds, roasted
- 25g hazelnuts, roasted

- White wine, to taste
- Red wine vinegar, to taste

1 Preheat the oven to 220C/gas 7. If you're using nora chillies, place them in a bowl then cover with boiling water. After 30 minutes, when softened, drain the chillies, chop them and bash into using a pestle and mortar. Set aside.
2 Place the pepper on a tray and roast till soft and blackened outside, about 30 minutes. When the pepper is cooked, place it in a bowl and cover with clingfilm. Leave to cool – the steam will help loosen the skin, so you can peel it easily.
3 Heat a drizzle of oil in a frying pan on a medium-low heat, then fry the bread on each side till golden and crisp. Remove from the pan, let cool, then finely chop.
4 Sauté the onion with a pinch of salt in a little oil till soft; add the tomato and a splash of water. Bring to the boil; simmer for 15 minutes till sweet and thickened.
5 In a mortar, pound the garlic with a pinch of salt till smooth. Bash in the nuts, till the texture of coarse sand. Bash in the peeled pepper to incorporate, then stir in the tomato, chillies or paprikas and bread. (You can also use a food processor.)
6 Add a splash of wine and vinegar, followed by a little water, till you have a coarse sauce. Taste for seasoning, then serve with grilled chicken or seafood. Refrigerate leftovers for up to 2 days.

CHIMICHURRI SAUCE

Makes about 450g

- 2 tomatoes, peeled, deseeded and finely chopped
- 1 red onion, finely chopped
- 3 garlic cloves, finely chopped
- A handful of parsley, chopped
- 1 tsp each dried oregano, chilli powder, paprika, ground cumin
- 1 bay leaf, finely chopped
- 8 tbsp olive oil
- 4 tbsp red wine vinegar

1 Combine all the ingredients in a bowl. Season to taste and serve with steak.

PINEAPPLE SALSA

Delicious with pork steaks or squid, hot from the barbecue.
Makes about 230g

- ½ tsp black mustard seeds
- ½ red chilli
- Olive oil
- 227g tinned pineapple rings in juice, chopped, juice reserved
- ½ lime

1 Fry the mustard seeds and chilli in a little oil over a medium-high heat. When fragrant, add the pineapple and juice, and pinch of pepper. Cook for 5 minutes, till thick and sticky. Squeeze in the lime, then put in a serving bowl.

ROMESCO SAUCE

RUNNER BEAN CHUTNEY

MIXED PEPPER OIL
Serve drizzled over steaks.
Makes 150ml
- 1 tbsp each of green, pink and black peppercorns
- 150ml olive oil
- A small bunch of parsley, chopped

1 Bash the peppercorns in a pestle and mortar. Gently heat the oil, then take off the heat and add the peppercorns and parsley. Leave to infuse and cool.

RUNNER BEAN CHUTNEY
Makes about 900g
- 1 onion, sliced
- 1 tbsp olive oil
- 600g runner beans, cut in 2cm pieces
- 2 tbsp mustard seeds
- 3 tbsp coriander seeds
- 3cm ginger, grated
- 250ml cider vinegar
- 200g caster sugar

1 Fry the onion in the oil over a medium heat until soft. Add the beans, mustard and coriander seeds and ginger, then cook for a further 5 minutes. Stir in the vinegar and sugar, and slowly bring to the boil. Simmer for 20–30 minutes till thickened. Spoon into sterilised jars and store in the fridge for up to 2 weeks.

GRIBICHE
A classic cold sauce for steamed new potatoes, asparagus or white fish.
Makes about 150ml
- 1 hard-boiled egg, peeled
- 75ml olive oil
- 1 tsp dijon mustard
- 1 tbsp white wine vinegar
- 3 cornichons, finely sliced
- 1 tbsp each capers, chopped parsley and chopped tarragon

1 Remove the yolk from the egg and chop the white. Mash the yolk in the base of a bowl, then slowly add the oil, mashing to form an emulsion. Mix in the mustard, vinegar and add a pinch of salt. Stir in the egg white, cornichon, capers and herbs.

EASY BERRY JAM
This jam doesn't have much sugar, so has a fresh fruity, summery taste, but doesn't keep for long.
Makes about 800g
- 1kg raspberries
- Zest of 1 lemon, juice of ½
- 150g sugar

1 Place everything in a large pan. Use a masher to lightly scrunch the berries, so the sugar dissolves. Put the pan on a high heat and bring to a boil, then simmer over a medium heat for 15 minutes till thickened and a little reduced. (Skim the foam from the surface every 5 minutes.) Allow to cool, then spoon into sterilised jars and refrigerate for up to a week.

BERRY-BASIL COULIS
Delicious on plain cheesecake or vanilla ice cream.
Makes about 250ml
- 250g strawberries, or other berries
- 8 large basil leaves
- A squeeze of lemon juice
- 1 tbsp icing sugar

1 In a blender, blitz everything till very smooth. Strain, and chill till ready to use.

GINGER CUSTARD
Pour generously over fruit crumbles.
Makes about 600ml
- 450ml milk
- 50ml double cream
- 6 egg yolks
- 50g sugar
- 2 tsp powdered ginger
- 1 tbsp cornflour

1 Pour the milk and cream into a pan over a medium heat. Whisk the egg yolks, sugar, powdered ginger and cornflour together in a bowl till smooth. As soon as the milk bubbles around the edge, pour it into the yolk mix, whisking all the time. Return the lot to the pan and place over a medium heat. Stir with a spatula till it thickens, then pour into a warmed jug.

EASY BERRY JAM

YEARBOOK INDEX

Editor
Andy Harris

Managing editor
Paul Dring

Deputy editor
Holly O'Neill

Art director
Adrienne Pitts

Deputy art director
Helen Little

Editorial assistant
Olivia Haughton, Clare Knivett

Editor at large
Jamie Oliver

Recipes
Stephanie Alexander, Fifteen London, Laura Fyfe,
Chris Gates, Andy Harris, Lloyd Hayes,
Maria Helm Sinskey, Joss Herd, Cara Hobday,
Honeybuns, Jamie's Italian, Anna Jones, Jeremy Lee,
Georgia Levy, Kate McCullough, Christina Mackenzie,
Jamie Oliver, Dinu Patel, Rena Patel, Rebecca Rauter,
Ginny Rolfe, Georgie Socratous, Phillippa Spence,
Sarah Tildesley, Union Jacks

Photography & illustration
Jan Baldwin , Laura Edwards, Tara Fisher,
Jonathan Gregson, Will Heap, Amanda Heywood,
Dan Jones, Emma Lee, David Loftus,
Andrew Montgomery, David Munns, Myles New,
Con Poulos, Sam Robinson, Anders Schønnemann,
Maja Smend, Becca Stadtlander, Sam Stowell,
Yuki Sugiura, Kate Whitaker

Advertising
Nancy Phillips, John Brown Media, 020 7565 6575
nancy.phillips@johnbrownmedia.com

Jamie Oliver Ltd
CEO John Jackson
Managing director Tara Donovan
Finance manager John Dewar
Finance manager Therese MacDermott
Management accountant Tenzin Gonkatsang
Head of legal Giovanna Milia

Subscriptions Jamie Magazine, Regal Place,
Maxwell Road, London SW6 2HD. ME9 8GU
020 7814 5064, jamie@subscriptions-mps.co.uk

For subscription enquiries in Australia and New Zealand,
email customercare@mymagazinesubscription.com.au or
telephone +61 1300 716 426. Postal enquiries can be
directed to Jamie Magazine, Locked Bag 527,
Frenchs Forest, NSW, 2086, Australia.

Distribution by Mail Publisher Solutions, Northcliffe House,
2 Derry Street, London W8 5TT, +44 20 3615 2790

Jamie Magazine is published by Jamie Magazine Ltd. Registered
Office 19–21 Nile Street, London N1 7LL, UK; 020 3375 5601.
Jamie is a registered trademark. Copyright 2012 Jamie Magazine
Ltd. Any reproduction without permission is prohibited. Jamie
Magazine contains editorial content from external contributors,
which does not necessarily reflect the views
of Jamie Magazine Ltd. Jamie Magazine does not accept or respond
to unsolicited manuscripts and photographs. The publishers do
not accept responsibility for errors in advertisements or
third-party offers. Jamie Magazine is printed in the UK by
Southernprint Ltd. Print management & reprographic services
by John Brown.

Member of the Audit Bureau of Circulations

GUIDELINE DAILY AMOUNTS

	Women	Men
Energy (Calories)	2000	2500
Protein (g)	45	55
Carbohydrate (g)	230	300
of which sugars (g)	90	120
Fat (g)	70	95
of which saturates (g)	20	30
Fibre (AOAC) (g)	24	24
Sodium (g)	2.4	2.4
Equivalent as salt (g)	6	6

People vary in many ways, such as size and activity levels. GDAs cannot be used as targets for individuals; they simply provide a benchmark against which contribution from nutrients per serving of foods can be roughly assessed. **These figures apply in the UK only.**

LIQUID

1 teaspoon	5ml
1 dessertspoon	12ml
1 tablespoon	15ml
1 shot	25ml
1 small wineglass	125ml
1 large wineglass	250ml
1 fl oz	30ml
1 pint	568ml
1 glug	about 20ml

OVEN TEMPERATURES

Celsius	Fahrenheit	Gas Mark
110C	225F	¼
130C	250F	½
140C	275F	1
150C	300F	2
170C	325F	3
180C	350F	4
190C	375F	5
200C	400F	6
220C	425F	7
230C	450F	8

For fan-assisted ovens, reduce temperatures by 10-20C

WEIGHT

Imperial	Metric
1oz	28g
1lb	450g

CUP MEASURES

	US	AUS
1 cup sugar	200g	220g
1 cup flour	115g	125g
1 cup liquid	240ml	250ml

Useful information

Ingredients

- We use Freedom Foods certified, free-range or organic pork and chicken and their by-products.

- Whenever possible, we look for sustainably managed fish, with an MSC or Freedom Foods mark.

- Unless otherwise specified, our recipes are tested with semi-skimmed milk, golden caster sugar, unsalted butter and large free-range eggs (average weight 60g).

- Unless otherwise specified, all herbs in recipes are fresh; we season with freshly ground black pepper and sea salt flakes; vegetables and fruit are washed and trimmed, and root vegetables such as onions, carrots, potatoes, garlic and ginger are peeled.

Cooking tips

- Our recipes are tested in conventional ovens, using oven thermometers. If you're using a fan-assisted oven, we advise reducing the temperature by 10-20C.

- To sterilise a jar, wash the jar and lid (removing the rubber seal, if there is one); place in an oven at 100C/gas ¼ for 30 minutes, until completely dry. Simmer the rubber seal in boiling water for 10 minutes; remove with tongs.

- We test cakes are done by inserting a metal skewer into the centre: if the skewer emerges clean and dry, the cake is cooked.

- Blind baking ensures pastry cases are cooked through. Line the pastry case with baking paper, fill with dried beans, rice or ceramic 'baking beans' and bake until pale golden. Remove the paper and beans and continue to cook the case further until light brown.

- Take extra care when boiling sugar or heating oil for deep-frying. Use appropriate thermometers, and never have children or pets in the kitchen when you do this.

- When creaming butter and sugar for cakes, aim for a very pale colour and a light, fluffy consistency. You may find it's easiest to use an electric whisk, beaters or mixer.

- To skin tomatoes or peaches: cut a tiny cross in the base, place in a bowl and cover with boiling water. Leave for a few minutes, then drain. When they're cool enough to handle (but still warm), the skin should peel off.

- Beansprouts have been linked to salmonella. Buy packets marked "ready to eat", otherwise they should be cooked through before eating.

- If cooking for people on a gluten-free or vegetarian diet, check ingredient labels carefully.